THE GENTLE
REBEL

THE GENTLE
REBEL

To Susan
with best wishes
for life-long success
and happiness
June x

June Picken

HISTORY INTO PRINT

First published by
History into Print, 56 Alcester Road,
Studley, Warwickshire B80 7LG in 2007
www.history-into-print.com

ISBN: 978 1 85858 318 1

A Cataloguing in Publication Record
for this title is available from the British Library

Typeset in Garamond
Printed in Great Britain by
Cromwell Press Ltd.

The Gentle Rebel

To my family...

❧ *The Gentle Rebel* ❧

"This child – she's asking those questions again!"

As I looked at my Dad's face I knew that whatever he said next would not be what I wanted to hear. I tightened my grip on the stuffed toy that I loved so much and glanced at Mom. He would turn to her for help as usual – she was always there – advising – reassuring and comforting, the solid anchor of my child life. She looked at me and smiled, and my heart slowed a little.

My dad appeared and disappeared like a shadow, never at home long enough for me to understand or know him well. He rarely sat and talked to me, but conversations between Mom, aunts and uncles, Dad himself and his ex-soldier friends had showed me quite early on that he was obsessed with the war which had ended in 1918. When he was in the house, military music blared out from the tall, black wind-up gramophone which stood near the window, as loud as if the band itself was in the room! Dad always sat in his cane-sided armchair banging his fists on the carved wooden arms, in time to the marching rhythm. I hated the sound – it was to me the knell of doom.

Now, as he sat in that same chair, I asked my question again, determined that one day I would get an answer, if not from my father then from someone else. If not today, then some day. I took a deep breath.

"Dad, will I ever see Jesus?"

There has to be a point of departure for any story so I'll begin, not at the age when I started asking questions but earlier, when my baby life ended and school life began…

As Mom turned the key in the lock of the back door I stood with John's pram at the end of the yard, near the tall, wooden gate, waiting for her signal that I should lift the latch. I looked hopefully up to Peter's bedroom window next door but it was dark, the curtain not moving. I had hoped he would wave to me as I set off for school on my first day. Earlier, I'd stood in front of the long mirror of the wardrobe in my parents' bedroom, wondering about the children I would soon be meeting. I didn't know many, only my baby brother John, a few cousins who lived on the other side of Birmingham, Fay and Clem Hatto at the garage further along Wardwards Lane and Marg Smith, my friend, who lived down the hill with her strange sister, Olive. Their parents seemed so much older than mine.

"Hurry up June! We've got to speak to Paddy yet!"

Mom had called me June. So… I was not Junie anymore. I was five years old… and grown up.

My clumsy fingers had tried to tie a bow in the cord of my woollen dress which Mom had knitted for me for this special day. It had a patterned skirt and a plain bodice with a row of holes round the waist where the cord was threaded through. Hearing Mom's voice, I'd given up trying to tie the bow and had made my way onto the small landing, peering down into the darkness. I'd called,

"Mom, I can't see to get down!"

I had never liked the staircase, each stair lino-covered like the landing, each one a challenge. Opening the door below a little wider, Mom let a shaft of light creep up towards me.

"Come on then!"

Cautiously I'd put a shoeless foot on the first stair, my hand feeling for the rail.

In the living room below John had sat patiently in his pram, secured by his harness, his blond hair curling round his chubby little face. Mom had helped me on with my new shoes, my sensible, lace up shoes. How I longed for some shiny black ankle strap ones like Fay's! But I was regarded as a tomboy – no fancy shoes for June, Dad had said. I'd put on my blue coat and Mom had given me a hankie for my pocket and a red apple for playtime. My new teacher, Miss Herring had told us that there would be milk to drink. Fay said it came in small bottles with a straw to drink it through and there was cream on the top! I would enjoy that!

Now, as I waited, Mom came towards me and I lifted the latch of the gate, still looking hopefully towards Peter's window. But he was not there. I wheeled the pram into the passage which divided the house – yards from the gardens which led to the entry while Mom closed the gate behind us.

"Mom, can I see Peter when I come home?"

Her face was serious. "I don't know, love. He's not well. Doctor Renwick is coming this morning."

My heart beat a tattoo of anxiety and I felt that by starting school I was deserting my sweetheart. Peter had a special teacher who came to the house. He could not attend an ordinary school because he had spent his fourteen years in a pram and a wheelchair, his thin legs encased in iron callipers. We had a special affinity, Peter and I, and he had a special song of the day which he'd adapted for me… 'If I Had a Talking Picture of Junie.' Sometimes when I was visiting him I had to go home again because he would suddenly stop talking, lean back in his wheelchair and bite his fingers, crying bitterly, lost to the world. I knew that as soon as I left Mrs Sargent would have to re-bandage those poor fingers with the strips of cream-coloured rag which had become so familiar to us all.

We reached the end of the passage and the small wooden gate which led into the yard of the house where my Godmother lived with her son Norman. Gip, the big Airedale dog, as tall as the gate, looked at me then kissed me.

"You're really ready for school, my love, aren't you?"

I nodded and stood quiet while Mom had a word with her, then I turned and ran out into the entry which divided the blocks of houses into fours. I shouted 'hello.o.o' and the curved roof took my voice and threw it down in a jumble of sound. Mom was calling "Wait! Don't go on the road!"

I turned and she caught me up, taking my hand. Presently we were passing Faye's Dad's garage where my Dad kept his car. Sometimes, Fay who was nine years old would ask me to play on the piles of car tyres at the back of the garage, or her Dad would let the two of us and Clem, her older brother, lick and seal envelopes in the office. I liked the bitter-sweet taste of the gum on the flaps but Mom disapproved.

"Her Dad could at least give a saucer of water and some cotton wool to do the job with. It's not hygienic!"

I'd asked what hygienic meant and she had explained. I liked learning new words!

Fay's home was topsy-turvy, with the office, bathroom and toilet on the ground floor, the living room, bedrooms and a sitting room above. Mom had often said "Fancy having to carry buckets of coal upstairs in winter! I wouldn't like that!" But recently the family had had gas fires put in upstairs, quite a luxury in Mom's eyes.

On Raddlebarn Road, which Mom called the Main Road, we approached the short row of houses and the shops. Billy, the milkman's horse was standing quietly with the cart, and as Mr Walters the milkman appeared from one of the houses Billy moved on a few steps, his hooves clip-clopping on the road.

"Isn't he clever?" I said to Mr Walters. "He knows just when to go!"

"Yes, he's clever alright, June. And what about you then? Are you off to school at last?" He beamed down at me and I nodded, looking at the horse, longing to stroke him.

Mom said, "As it's her first day I'm coming with her. Will you leave me a pint with Mrs Plimmer, Mr Walters please? She's got my jug. I'll pay you tomorrow if that's all right."

He nodded, "I'll be there in a while. Good luck, Junie."

He moved on and so did we, reaching the shops. Mom said, "As it's your first day you can have a penny to spend at Mrs Cameron's."

"Oh!" I gasped with delight, dashing past the chemist's shop to look in Mrs Cameron's window. Mom laughed and called "This afternoon I mean! Not now! Come on, we must speak to Paddy before you go into school!"

We passed the Post Office and reached the corner of Gristhorpe Road where Paddy, the big Irish policeman stood surrounded by children, all fighting to hold his hand. I looked at him with awe. He was so huge compared with Dad, and even the tallest of my uncles, Uncle Jack, who was hoping to join the Scots Guards. Mom had told me that Paddy loved children and that was why he was always on duty at the school corner. I knew I would have to be quick if I was to be first to cross the road with him at dinnertimes.

"Good morning Paddy" Mom called above the din. His blue eyes lit up. "Good morning to ye, Missus."

Mom put an arm round my shoulders. "June's starting school today. Will you please watch for her at dinnertime? I shall be here to meet her this afternoon."

"I will, to be sure." He looked down at me and I said brightly "I'm going to have a penny to spend."

"Ah mavourneen" he said in his lilting Irish brogue, "If I could be let loose in that lovely shop of Mrs Cameron's sure and I'd eat every sweetie there!"

I must have looked shocked and he laughed. "I'll watch out for her, don't ye worry."

His face crumpled into a thousand laughter lines as he ruffled my well-brushed curly hair. More children gathered, jealous of his attention to us. He addressed the crowd in a loud voice.

"Now listen all of yez! Stand on the kerb here till I says go! Then ye keep close to me heels till we're across to the other side! Do yez understand what oi'm saying?"

They all shouted 'yes' and Mom and I crossed with the crowd, accompanied by Paddy. There was always some traffic on Raddlebarn Road - cars, motorcycles with sidecars, horse-drawn carts like Mr Walters' milk cart, an occasional coal cart. Sometimes there was a bread van and the driver would bring out a basket full of loaves, although Mom bought our bread from Mr Bonnell's bakery which stood on the corner of Hubert Road. Mr Bonnell only had one arm. He'd been run over by a car outside his shop and one arm had to be taken off at the hospital.

We walked down Gristhorpe Road, passed the school caretaker's house and the long row of black railings to where the main gate stood open. This was the entrance to the Junior School and where I had to go in on my first day. The Infants School entrance was further down the road, next to my favourite park Muntz Park.

Mom gave me a hug and a kiss. "I'd better get back, love. I don't like leaving John for too long. He starts showing off. See if you can find Fay or Marge."

I nodded, feeling suddenly alone and a little afraid.

"Don't forget - keep close to Paddy at dinnertime. Hold his hand if you can." I could see tears in Mom's eyes and I nearly cried myself. I had loved being at home but I wanted to learn writing and sums. I wanted to learn everything there was to learn... and I wanted to find out what Jesus looked like...

Mom left and I looked round the playground for familiar faces but there was nobody I knew. Then the Bull sounded, making me jump almost out of my skin. Clem, Fay's brother, who was eleven, had told me that there was a real live bull up there in the dome on the school roof, fighting to get out and that was why it made such a noise!

"New children over here please... and no talking!" A stern voice called and I saw a tall lady dressed in a brown tweed skirt and green jumper standing near the school door, holding a piece of paper and a pencil.

"Form a queue... and no talking, I said!" Presently, as we shuffled into the school some older children came close, grinning and pulling faces at us. The teacher told them off and they moved away.

Inside the building I had an impression of immense space. The ceilings were high, the wall painted pale green halfway down, then there were brown tiles reaching the skirting boards. We passed the Juniors' cloakroom and I could see rows of silver-coloured pegs. Presently we were walking through the assembly hall, its parquet floor gleaming with polish like a golden sea. Wall windows were set so high that I could only see sky outside. There was a row of classrooms to our right and further on was the Infants section. The stern teacher announced "Miss Brady wants you all in the classroom now. You'll hang up your coats later." Miss Brady! The name went round like wildfire. Where was our teacher, Miss Herring? I had met Miss Herring, a plump, ginger-haired lady with a freckled face. She had stopped to speak to us one day. She had looked at me and "You will enjoy school my dear, I'm sure. You will be in my class to begin with." Now, what had gone wrong? Where was Miss Herring?

A door opened and a woman, dressed all in black, came out. Her iron-grey hair was drawn back into a bun and her dark eyes glittered behind horn-rimmed spectacles.

"I am Miss Brady," she boomed. "I am your Headmistress. Miss Herring is not well so I shall be your teacher for today, perhaps longer. Now, into the classroom so that I can call the register!"

I felt close to tears. I didn't like the look of this lady at all. There was a flurry as everybody jostled for seats. The desks stood in rows, each with a seat to hold two children and there were gangways between the rows. I found myself sitting with a girl in a blue dress and she had a slide in her brown hair. I saw with some satisfaction that she had on sensible shoes like mine. She looked at me with wide eyes and I think she was a bit scared.

"I'm June," I whispered but she didn't answer. The desk had a lift-up top and I put my apple inside. I could smell furniture polish and there were numbers and letters scratched into the desk top. A white crock inkwell sat in the right top corner and I was suddenly excited. Were we going to write with a pen so soon? But when I leaned over and looked into the inkwell I could see that there was no ink in it. After Miss Brady had done the register she took us to the cloakroom.

"Choose a peg and remember the number. You will always use the same peg while you are in this part of the school. The same will apply to you when you go up to the Juniors. No changing about!"

During the morning the Headmistress wrote the alphabet on the big blackboard which sat on an easel at the front of the class and later she taught us a hymn, 'All Things Bright and Beautiful.' My heart lifted a little. She could certainly play the piano and seemed to enjoy that more than anything. At playtime a bell rang and she took us out to the small playground. Dorothy, my desk-mate and I peered through some railings.

"It's the park." I said excitedly to Dorothy. "My favourite park!"

"And mine" she said.

Then we heard loud voices coming from behind the high wall which ran along the back of the playground. Somebody said, "The big boys school is there" so Dorothy and I moved away, worried that some of the big boys might appear on top of the wall. We played for a while then discovered a drinking fountain. It became the object of great interest, tall and white, with a bowl on top and in the centre of the bowl a hole for water to come through. The teacher on playground duty pressed a button at the side and a jet of water came up. We all took it in turns to have a drink. When she moved away a boy pressed the button for a girl and pushed her face into it. She burst into tears and the teacher came back, cuffed the boy's ear and moved us all away from the drinking fountain.

After play I felt quite relaxed. Back at our desk I began to tell Dorothy about Fay's Dad's garage and how we played on the piles of tyres....

"That girl in the green dress – come out here!"

There was a hush and everyone looked round. I realised with horror that Miss Brady meant me!

"Yes – you miss!"

I got out of my seat and walked between the rows of desks, feeling very self-conscious. Somebody giggled and as I stood in front of the figure in black I decided that Miss Brady was a witch!

"Don't stare at me like that, young lady! You may be only five years old but I expect obedience!"

She turned and walked to a large wooden cupboard, which stood behind the blackboard and easel. Opening the door she took out a cane with a curved handle. A murmur ran round the classroom and I was indignant. What had I done to deserve punishment?

"Your hands, miss." She grabbed one of my hands and turned it palm up, then the other. Swish! Down came the cane, one stroke on each palm. I pressed my lips together, grimly deciding not to cry.

"Back to your desk and no more talking!" Miss Brady shouted at me, glaring round the classroom.

"That goes for all of you... and stop that giggling!"

My hands were burning as I walked back to our desk. A boy put his foot out to try and trip me up, then as I sat down my nose began to bleed! Dorothy put up a hand. "Please, miss, her nose is bleeding!"

Miss Brady tut-tutted. "Oh dear… you'd better lie under the desk. Have you got a hankie?"

I put my hand to my nose and got blood all over it.

"It's in my coat pocket in the cloakroom." I said timidly.

She took a piece of cloth from a drawer and brought it over. "Use this. It's only had chalk on it. Lie down… quickly!" I took the cloth and got down under the desk, more worried about my new dress than the nose bleed, for I often had them. Dorothy looked down at me sympathetically. What a beginning, I thought. Caning and a nose bleed! It would be something to tell Peter when I got home, anyway, if I was able to see him. I put my hand up, wondering if I was doing the right thing.

"Please miss, Mom puts a big key down my back when my nose bleeds at home."

She stared at me and muttered "Just… stay as you are."

Presently the bleeding stopped and I struggled into my seat. I clutched the bloody cloth, not knowing what to do with it. Dorothy lifted the desk top and I put it inside. Then I remembered my apple was there so I moved the cloth to one side.

Miss Brady didn't look at me again then said, "Now listen, all of you, make sure you come back with clean hands this afternoon. We shall be looking at books and if there's time we shall learn another hymn."

At dinnertime the bull sounded, making me jump again. We hurried to the cloakroom to get our coats and I managed to be first out of the door. Outside I hurried through the small gate, up the hill, passed the Juniors' gate, to the corner where Paddy stood on duty.

"Ah mavourneen, you're going to be a quick one I can see!" He held out his hand and I took it shyly, walking close to him, my new symbol of security. I could smell tobacco, leather and metal polish, and as I looked up at his helmet I was a little afraid of the spike on top of it. I thanked him as we reached the other side, then I ran past the shops and houses, to the corner of our road, Wardwards Lane, deciding not to tell Mom about the caning I'd had. I reached home and Mom kissed me. John was sitting in his high chair and waved his hand at me. A red mark had appeared on both of mine.... I should have kept them hidden...

"Did you enjoy your first morning, then?" Mom asked.

I nodded. "We learned a hymn and we're going to look at books this afternoon. When can I go and see Peter, Mom?"

Mom's face was very serious. "Peter's got to rest, June. That means no visitors for a few days. You'll have to be patient."

My heart leapt with worry and panic. If I didn't go and see Peter he would think I didn't want to bother with him any more. I was close to tears.

"I want to go and see Peter!"

She put an arm round me. "Wash your hands and sit at the table. It's your favourite dinner – curried beef and rice."

I didn't want to eat. All I could think of was Peter, my sweetheart. My world was suddenly falling apart, my comfortable secure world of family and friends, pastimes and pleasures, fading away! I said shakily "I don't want to go back to school."

Mom tut-tutted. "Don't be silly! It's only because you can't go next door isn't it? She hesitated then said "Look, I'll try and see Mrs Sargent this afternoon. She may let you see him for just a few minutes. But if he's been biting his fingers..."

She stopped and I thought of Peter's poor fingers encased in the strips of rag, so often washed and dried again, freed of blood. I had never understood why he bit his fingers – he was so clever, so kind and funny in between the terrible moments...

"He's a loony." Clem had said one day scornfully.

"I don't know why you bother with him."

"He's my sweetheart." I'd said innocently, and he had laughed in a cruel way and pulled a face at me.

I ate my dinner, more to please Mom than anything. Afterwards, I put on my pumps and went to play in the yard, opening the lavatory door to take my skipping rope from the hook there. I played for a while, trying not to make too much noise because of Peter.

Later Mom told me to wash my hands again and said kindly, "John and I will meet you this afternoon then you can have your penny to spend."

I looked at her fearfully. "But what about Peter?"

She said "I'll see his Mom if I can. I know how badly you want to see him and tell him about your first day."

My heart lifted a little, and back at school Miss Brady went round looking at our hands, before letting us see the books. She seemed to hesitate when she looked at mine. The red marks were still there.

Later she taught us 'There is a Green Hill Far Away Without a City Wall' explaining that the green hill was where the cross had been put up on which Jesus was crucified. When I thought about it I seemed to have such a pain in my chest. It seemed so cruel a punishment. I didn't understand what 'without a city wall' meant in the hymn, but perhaps Miss Brady would explain one day.

I put up my hand cautiously, knowing that I was not exactly one of her favourites.

"Is there a photograph of Jesus?" My heart was beating fast and she stared at me.

"Don't be silly, child! It was too long ago for photography. All we have to go on are paintings done by people who have had visions of Jesus, or who have painted Him from their imagination."

I didn't understand what she meant but I would ask Mom. Dad always said I asked too many questions but my mind was bustling with questions. I wanted to learn about everything in the world, and everything about Jesus… and what He looked like.

"She's too nosey for her own good!" Dad said often. "Five years old… I ask you!"

Mom defended me. "She's eager to learn - you should be pleased, Will."

He had grunted and carried on reading his newspaper. That's all he ever seemed to do, or he'd sit at his big desk writing, or listening to his records of military bands. When he was out Mom would play her own records - Rio Rita, Ramona, Body and Soul, After the Ball… When I remarked about Dad's records she would smile and say "He does like dance music as well. Why else would he have a dance band?" I knew about the dance band. It was called The Esmerelda and was one of the reasons why Dad was out a lot, and didn't often see me before I went to bed.

The afternoon had gone quickly and as I stood ready to go to the cloakroom Miss Brady's voice whispered in my ear -

"June Keppy - just a minute."

Now what had I done wrong? She was pressing something into my hand and saying 'For not crying this morning.'

I went to the cloakroom and collected my coat, then I stood by the wall outside and looked into my hand. Two toffees lay there, wrapped in red and gold paper! I stared at them, puzzled, put them into my coat pocket and slipped the coat on. Mom was waiting at the small gate with John. She kissed me and I touched John's hand.

"I'll give you the penny when we've crossed the road," she said. We reached Paddy's corner, saw that he was busy so we gave him a wave. On the other side of the road Mom handed me a penny and I ran to Mrs Cameron's shop. Excitedly I pushed open the door, the bell jangling above my head. Mrs Cameron came out from the back, dressed in her flowered overall.

Grey-haired and rosy cheeked, she spoke with a strange accent which Dad said was Scottish. Scotland was his own favourite country, though he had travelled to many in his youth. "We'll all go together one day" he had promised, "and I'll show you a real castle, like the one painted on my big drum."

"Did you enjoy your first day, lassie?" Mrs Cameron asked. I nodded and held up the penny.

"I've got a penny to spend today," I said "because it's my first day at school."

"Oh, you are lucky!" she exclaimed. "Take your time choosing then, while I go and speak to your Mummy."

She went out and I looked into the window where the open boxes of sweets lay, a kaleidoscope of colours and shapes. I wanted everything I could see!

There were aniseed balls, gobstoppers, pear drops, coconut flakes, packets of coconut tobacco, love hearts, fruit lumps, chocolate chewing nuts, marzipan teacakes, peas and potato, pink and white sugar coated fish, surprise bags, tiger nuts, liquorice root, dolly mixtures, acid drops, dabs and suckers, sherbet fountains, wine gums, American gums, toasted teacakes, Pontefract cakes, liquorice whirls and bootlaces. At last I decided to have brightly coloured love hearts, a dab and a sucker which was a triangular bag of sherbet, with a liquorice tube in one corner and a stick with toffee in the other.

Mrs Cameron came back into the shop. "I've had a nice wee chat with your Mummy. Have you made up your mind, lassie?"

I told her my choice and as she weighed out the love hearts, I said, "I didn't know what to choose." I gave her the penny and she smiled as she handed me the little white bag and a dab and a sucker. I put both items in my coat pocket. We said goodbye and I went out. John's pram was outside the chemist shop and Mom was inside buying Spanish juice. It was a kind of liquorice, hard and thick which had to be broken with a hammer although sometimes she would give a stick to suck 'For your bowels' she would say.

Mr Palethorpe, the chemist, was tall and thin and wore a white coat. He peered at me through this metal-rimmed spectacles.

"Well, Junie, did you finish that jigsaw puzzle I gave you?"

I nodded. "It was a bit hard. Dad helped me."

He continued, "You understand about the ivory castles being your teeth, don't you, and Giant Decay being the enemy of your teeth."

"Enemy?" I was puzzled and he laughed.

"It's what destroys your teeth, eating too many sweets and not cleaning them every day."

I nodded, thinking about the toothpaste, Gibbs Dentifrice. It came in pink or blue tins and was like a little cake, wrapped in crinkly see-through paper. I always managed to get some of the paper in my mouth whenever I rubbed my toothbrush on the paste. Presently we made our way home and at the top of the entry Gip was standing at the gate, wagging his tail furiously.

"Mom, he knew we were coming! Isn't he clever?"

The big dog licked my hands and strangely, they didn't feel so sore. Godmother came out of the houses wheeling John's pram.

"Well then my love, did you enjoy your first day at school?"

I nodded, stoking Gip's wiry fur. I opened the gate for Mom to push the pram out into the passage. Mom said, "Come and have a cup of tea, Nell." Godmother nodded and smiled at me. "June, I've cooked some of those tiny potatoes you like. I'll bring a few with me."

As we approached our gate I said with some desperation, "I want to see Peter, Mom."

"No... it can't be today."

My heart dropped and I felt close to tears. I wanted so much to see him and tell him about the caning and the nosebleed.

"Open the gate for me, June."

I obeyed and stood looking up towards Peter's bedroom window again. Where was he? What was happening to him?

Mom unlocked the back door after parking the pram. She looked at me "When Godmother comes in you can tell us all about your first day, can't you? I'll put the kettle on. Talk to John a few minutes."

Godmother arrived with a small basin full of little steaming potatoes glistening with butter. She speared two on the fork she'd brought with her and offered them to me. My mouth closed joyously over them and I tasted the saltiness of the butter. Mom brought the tray in with the tea and some bun loaf, also some butter.

"Nell, you'll never guess! This child was drinking vinegar in the pantry yesterday!"

Godmother smiled and pretended to be shocked.

"Oh dear, it will shrivel your tummy! You don't like coal as well, do you Junie?"

"Oh no!" I shook my head vigorously. I couldn't imagine doing that!

That night Dad came home earlier than usual and Mom said in the kitchen, "Dad will want to hear all about it but leave it till he's had his tea."

I gulped, my heart fluttering with guilt and anxiety. I knew I should never tell lies but how could I tell him, or Mom, everything? I'd already decided to keep quiet about the caning, and I hadn't yet mentioned the nosebleed to Mom.

After tea Dad sat in his chair and looked at me with his vivid blue eyes, "Tell me about your first day at school, then, child."

I hesitated then related the day's events, carefully including the nosebleed but not the caning. Mom said, "You didn't tell me your nose had bled." I said casually, "Miss Brady gave me a piece of rag for it. I put it in my desk after."

She looked surprised. "Miss Brady?"

I nodded, "Miss Herring is poorly. Miss Brady is teaching us till she is better."

Dad nodded towards me. "She's got a good brain, this child. She remembers everything in detail."

I sat beside his chair on the floor, poking my fingers through the cane-work. He looked down at me.

"I don't want you going to that awful school down the road. You'll go to a secondary or a grammar school and maybe university, get a degree."

Mom protested, "She won't understand all that, Will."

I didn't want to understand. I knew that if I went to another school other than the Senior Girls one I wouldn't see Fay or Marg again. Marg would have to go there as it was closer to her home and she was expected to look after her sister Olive, who was sixteen. Olive looked slightly Oriental, with her slanting eyes and dark fringed hair. Mom had said one day, "Olive is different to most children and you must never pass remarks about her to anybody, especially her family."

That night, after we had looked at one of Dad's 'Countries of the World' books I said, "Mom, when can I see Peter?"

"If he's well enough you may be able to see him tomorrow. Don't fret! Doctor Renwick knows what's best for him."

But I was fretting. I wanted to tell Peter everything... the caning, the nosebleed, everything. And I wanted to give him one of the toffees Miss Brady had given to me... for not crying... but I felt like crying. I was worried about my sweetheart.

I was becoming more aware of my home, and although I liked my own little bedroom I loved going into Mom's and Dad's room. It had flowered wallpaper on the walls, with a border along the top, down a bit from the ceiling, which was white. There was a window divided into two sections with a lock in the middle so that each section could be pulled up or down. There were flowered curtains and a piece of cream net halfway up the window. There was the dark oak wardrobe with the long mirror, a matching chest of drawers and a dressing table which had three hinged mirrors. The bedspread which Mom put on the bed in summer was blue and white, and on the underside it was still blue and white, with a different pattern. The shiny lino on the floor was fawn coloured, and there was a little green rug which my Auntie Floss, one of Mom's sisters had made for her. The gas fitting hung in the middle of the ceiling and didn't throw a shadow on the wall as mine did. There was a washstand with a pink bowl and jug, and a soap dish to match. A wooden clotheshorse stood nearby, with white towels on it.

John's cot stood near one wall but he would soon be having his own room. We were lucky - we had three bedrooms but no bathroom. It was Mom's ambition to have one, and Dad's ambition to have a garage for his car. There was a small fireplace in each of the three bedrooms, and when we were all in the living room, the door to the stairs was kept closed because a draught blew down the whole time. Dad had said he would block up the fire-grates, but Mom was firmly against that. "Don't do that, Will! If anyone is ill in bed a fire can be a comfort. Maybe one day we'll have gas fires."

Our living room overlooked the long, narrow, blue-bricked yard, the window the same shape as the bedroom one, with flowered curtains but no net. The table could be made bigger if Mom pulled out the two leaves, as she called them. There were four dining chairs, a sideboard, Dad's cane-sided armchair, Mom's chair and my own, made by my Uncle Frank, Mom's brother. He had also made the high chair for John which could be folded down. There were cupboards on each side of the black-leaded fireplace and I kept my toys in one of the bottom ones. I loved books, had rag books, pop-up books, magic painting books, a spinning top, a slate and chalks. On the sideboard with the family photos was a big stone jar of Virol, Cod Liver Oil and Malt, which I liked. Round the hearth was a brass fender with a little seat at each end, and a tall metal mesh fireguard in front of the fire. There was a pair of brass-backed bellows to liven up the fire, and a companion set stood to one side, with a brush, tongs, long-handled shovel and poker, all with matching top. Our kitchen had a wooden-rollered wringer, a washtub with a 'dolly' for moving the washing round, a crock sink and a wooden draining board. There was a large cupboard, a gas stove, and a table with a drawer at the front. Outside, next to the kitchen, was the coalhouse, then the 'lar' with its wooden seat from wall to wall. The lar was my refuge where I could sit and count the bricks on the walls. My own room overlooked the sloping roof, and beyond was the tall wooden gate leading out into the passage. A small gate led into each garden and beyond was a high wooden fence which ran right along the bottom of all the gardens. In ours we had foxgloves and ferns from the countryside, and Michaelmas daisies, in their seasons. Dad often said, "In spring we'll go in the car and find some rocks and I'll make a rockery." Mom had added, "Perhaps we'll find some sticky buds and catkins to put in a vase."

I was anxious to know what catkins were and she said, "Well, they're also called lambs' tails." I was still puzzled but longed to go into the countryside.

Once I was settled in at school time seemed to fly. We had learned the alphabet and done some writing in pencil on ruled paper. Miss Herring, thankfully, had come back after two days, and we didn't see much of Miss Brady after that except for hymn practice and assemblies.

We had been taken round to see some rabbits which lived in two hutches near the Juniors' cycle sheds. Miss Finucane, one of the Juniors' teachers had explained that they were Angora rabbits, and that some of the better-behaved Juniors took it in turns to look after them and comb them. The hair, she said, was sent away in brown paper bags for a good cause.

"What's a good cause?" I asked Mom. She'd laughed and said, "Everything I do is for a good cause" and when I told her about the rabbits' wool she nodded, "Oh yes, it raises money for charity. Jumpers are made from it." She ruffled my hair, "You and the family are my good cause - it's to do with love."

I'd been able to see Peter at last for a few minutes and was worried to see how pale and thin he looked. Mrs Sargent brought us both a glass of lemonade and, left us to talk.

I told him about being caned and he was shocked, "That was terrible, Junie! She shouldn't have done that to you! There had been tears in his eyes and I said in panic, "Don't tell your Mom, Peter. My Mom doesn't know, nor Dad!"

He began to get very upset and the inevitable happened - he leaned back in his wheelchair and bit his fingers in a long, drawn out, almost savage movement.

"It's my fault!" I sobbed as Mrs Sargent led me gently from the room.

"No dear, it's not. But I must tell you, June, Peter may have to go to a special hospital in London. I've told your Mummy."

My heart did a somersault. "Won't I see him anymore?"

She touched my cheek, "I hope you will. Perhaps your Mummy and Daddy could bring you in the car. We're looking for a house to rent near the hospital."

This was a double blow! I was very attached not only to Peter but to his parents too. I prayed that he might get better and not have to at all. I couldn't imagine my life without him...

Miss Herring said we should look at as many books as possible so Dad showed me some more of his, the 'Countries of the World' geography books some life stories of famous soldiers, stories by somebody called Dickens, had a set of war books bound in blue, but he would not open these for me to see the pictures. He also had two big books of plays by someone called Shakespeare with pictures in them. He told me that he had an ancestor called George Herbert who had been a poet. He explained the words to me and showed me a book of Latin verses by him.

"You'll be as clever as he was," Dad said, but I doubted it. In the front of the book was an illustration of George Herbert. He was dressed in dark clothes with a big white collar and a little cap on his head.

"He looks just like you, Dad, but he's got long hair."

He had laughed, "I wish I had his talent, child!"

Life revolved around school, home, the parks, Fay's Dad's garage and visits to relatives and friends. Granny Buttercup had said I could go and spend a week with her when I was older. A visit to Argyle Street in Nechells meant a game of cards with Grandad, and hearing my uncles play their various musical instruments. Uncle Jim, the youngest, drew pictures for me of sheiks, palm trees and pyramids and talked of someone called Rudolph Valentino. He had promised to teach me to play something called Jaws, or Jews Harp. It was a small musical instrument, which had to be pressed against the teeth, but I didn't like the idea. I wanted to take care of my teeth. I'd promised Mr Palethorpe I would. My Aunt Doll, Mom's youngest sister, showed me her latest fashion buys, including the pink satin nightie which Mom had often described in a story about a sparrow, which had always been my favourite.

"When you are older," Aunt Doll would say, "I'll take you to the pictures, and we can go to the Onion Fair when it comes."

"What's that?" I'd wanted to know.

"At the Serpentine Ground in Aston. It's a big fairground. Linegar will win you a coconut. She's good at that."

Linegar was Aunt Doll's best friend who worked with her at Lewis's Store in the centre of Birmingham. I was longing to be more adventurous – go on the tram to the Lickey Hills with my friends, and to the tuppenny crush at the Stirchley Pavilion on a Saturday morning. I longed to do a journey by tram. In some trams there was an open-ended curved seat on the upper deck, front and back, and friends told me they could hang on to the ironwork as the tram trundled along to the Lickey Hills. It sounded great fun!

On Sunday mornings Dad had begun to take me with him to see his Dad in another suburb of Birmingham. He was a strange man. He rarely spoke to me, just talked about the wars he'd been in and the war he was sure would come. Secretly I called him 'Grandad Beer' as there were always beer bottles on the table.

Dad said, "When you are older I'll tell you why he lives in Birmingham and Granny Camilla lives at the seaside. You might be able to spend a holiday with her sometime. I'll drop her a line."

That was something to look forward to, I thought, but Dad promised so many things…

On the way home he always called at a shop and bought a box of Kunzles chocolates for Mom. Sometimes Grandad Beer gave me a sixpence, but not very often!

Dad was very fond of his car, and my job was to wash the wheels for tuppence. The latest was called a 'Sunbeam' and was the talk of the road. It had little trays which folded into the backs of the two front seats, and for the people who sat in the back there were the foot rests which came out of the front seats too! There were even seats which folded into the two back doors of the car! Fay and Marg sometimes came and cleaned the rest of the car and Dad gave them sixpence each. If the Eldorado ice cream man cycled passed, Dad would buy us each a fruit water ice in a cardboard holder. Sometimes Clem would come and help but usually he decided he was too good to work with girls. He seemed to have plenty of pocket money anyway!

I enjoyed my days, but had begun to dread the nights. I had bad dreams, and the gas mantle threw a creepy shadow onto the wall, like a man in a long black cloak, wearing a big black hat. I'd told Mom and she said, "I'll get some nightlights. Mr Powell sells them, I'm sure."

That same night I was comforted by a squat little white candle in a yellow paper wrapper, set in a saucer of water, on my bedside cabinet.

Mom was always there for me despite being busy with John and my new baby sister Jacqueline. Mom helped Dad a lot, sorting the music out and keeping the drums cleaned. These were kept in the front parlour which we rarely used. The big drum had on its front the painting of a ruined Scottish castle, and there was a light inside. If I was good Dad would let me sit on a stool and bang the foot pedal against the back of the big drum, or tap the side drum with sticks. Sometimes he would let me crash the cymbals but Mom protested at the noise. John had been taken to the Photographic Studio in the Great Western Arcade to have his photograph taken. He was dressed in a cream shirt and blue velvet trousers, sitting on the same fur-covered box that I had sat on at his age. The two oval frames were then hung side by side above the fireplace in the parlour. As well as the drums there was a three-piece suite, a glass-fronted china cabinet, a carpet square and lino surround, and a green half-moon shaped rug, in front of the fireplace. A heavy curtain hung on the inside of the front door and Mom kept our every-day coats under it. The inner door was near the pantry and it led into the living room.

There was a tall black telephone on a small black table and it rang often, usually telling Dad he had to go out. I longed to speak into it but so far hadn't had the chance. Children at school envied us the 'phone, but Fay and Clem boasted that their Dad had two, one for the garage and one for the upstairs in their living quarters.

Dad said, "One day you'll learn French. You'll like that. It's useful to know a foreign language."

He said that he had Scottish and French on his side of the family, Welsh on Granny Camilla's side and Mom said she had Irish and Italian on hers!

Now that I was in Junior School I could play in the playground, and even take a turn in combing the Angora rabbits. I loved the local shops – Mr Powell's corner shop on the corner of Tiverton Road was a fairyland. Everything was in sacks, tubs, jars or boxes; butter was in large slabs, with wooden pots to shape the half pounds or pounds ordered by customers. What fascinated me was the way the money was sent to the cash office. Mr Powell put the money into a round box, attached it to a wire which was strung across the shop. The box travelled along this to the cash office where Mrs Powell took it down, and put the change, if any, into the box and sent it back to the counter.

Christmas was magic. I'd dreamed of having a doll's pram but it never materialised. But I did have a nice doll with real hair and eyelashes. One day John snatched it from me and cracked her head. He got smacked for that! Christmas Eve was a special time. John and I hung up a sock by the fireplace and went to bed early in a fever of excitement. On Christmas morning we found little gifts in the socks, and new pennies, nuts and an orange in our shoes. There were also pencils, chalks and pop-up or magic painting books to help us pass the time. Dad had bought me a nice wooden pencil box with a sliding lid which had flowers painted on it. Dad said it had been made in China. Inside was a pen, a pencil and a rubber, even a pencil sharpener.

Boxing Day meant a visit to Granny Buttercup's house where the whole family gathered happily every year. All the uncles did their party piece, playing the instrument of their choice. Most of them could play several instruments.

Dad was out most nights of the year with the dance band so I still didn't see him before going to bed. There had been more discussion about the club for ex-servicemen he wanted to start, and there had been a lot of activity at home with his various friends who wanted to help him.

I had begun going to Sunday school which was held in the green building next the Country Girl pub on Raddlebarn Road. We had sung the hymns I'd learned at school but I still needed the answer to a question.

"What does without a city wall mean Dad? We sing a hymn about it and Miss Brady says it's where Jesus was put on the cross. I wish I could go there."

He put down his newspaper and looked at me.

"You do say some funny things, child." He stood up and went to the door leading upstairs. "I'll show you something if you like."

Presently he came down carrying a black book.

"What's that?" I was breathless with excitement.

"You can hold it but be careful with it. The pages are very thin."

I took the book from him and gazed at it with wonderment. There were two words in gold 'Holy Bible.' The cover was of crinkly leather and the edges of the pages were all gold. I had never seen anything like it before!

"Look in the back section," Dad said, "there are pictures of some of the places you may be hearing about at Sunday school."

"Is there a picture of Jesus?" It was out before I could stop myself. I knew what the answer would be, that I would have to rely on paintings done from people's imagination, as Miss Brady had said. Dad didn't answer my question. I suppose he couldn't.

"It was given to me by your Godmother," he said, "when I became a Sunday School teacher."

I looked at him with surprise. I couldn't really imagine Dad as a Sunday School teacher!

He continued, "She gave it to me in 1921, that's three years before you were born. I met your Mom in 1922 and we got married. Have a look through it. It will be yours some day."

"Oh!" I was delighted with this news and my heart began to beat fast as I looked through the Bible. There were pictures of Jerusalem, Nazareth, Bethlehem, and Dad found for me the special hill where Jesus was crucified. My heart still ached as I looked at the place. There were pictures too of ruins, carvings, statues, and all kinds of exotic things including one of a man carrying something that looked like an animal on his back.

Dad explained, "He's a water seller. They used, and probably still do in some places, skins of animals to carry the water. No tins or bottles in those days! Oh, and 'without a city wall' means 'outside a city wall' but you have probably guessed that by now, from the picture."

"Yes," I said, "but why is Godmother called that? Is she God's mother?"

He smiled, "Of course not! I'll try and explain. When parents have a friend they have known a long time they choose him or her to take care of their child in case anything happens."

"In case anything happens?" I repeated, my heart quickening.

He nodded, "Yes, if anything happened to me or your Mom then Godmother Plimmer would take care of you. John has Uncle Frank and Auntie Jess as his Godparents, but we haven't decided about Jacqueline's yet."

I looked at the Bible again, enjoying the experience. Then Dad said, "Let me have it back now. Reluctantly I obeyed and as he went back upstairs with the Bible I thought how wonderful it was that some day it would be mine.

Dad had told me that there were lots of parks in Birmingham, not only my favourite, Muntz Park and the 'Rec' near home.

"Canon Hill Park has a boating lake," he said. "One day we'll go and have a boat out. There's a museum there. You'll like that."

"What's a museum?" I asked.

"It's a place where lots of interesting things are gathered together, on walls or in glass cases, old coins, old fashioned gadgets, paintings, that kind of thing."

"Paintings?" I picked up on this. "Would there be a painting of Jesus there?"

He rubbed his nose and I felt that he didn't know. Then he said, "I haven't been there for many years."

He continued, "Some parks have bandstands. In summer all kinds of bands play in them. Cannon Hill Park has one and Handsworth does too."

Muntz Park would always be my favourite park, even though there was no bandstand. There were swings and a maypole, and sheds for sheltering from the rain, but to me The Dell made the park special.

The Dell was a large hollow area in the middle of the park. It was bounded by railings, with sets of bush-lined steps leading from different places down to a dance area. This was for adults only. Children were not allowed to go down on their own, only with an adult. Mom often told me the story which I would always remember:

"At night," she'd say, "when the park is closed and every thing is quiet, a little sparrow stands on a special spot on the dance floor. The floor opens up and the sparrow goes down to fairyland with messages for the Fairy Princess who lives there." The description of the Princess's dress was often like my Aunt Doll's latest fashion buy. Sometimes it would be the nightie, pink satin with puffed sleeves, trimmed with lace, sometimes it was a blue velvet dress!

I'd always longed to run down one of the flights of steps and find the magic place. In the 'Rec' Fay, Marg, and I played together chewing sorrel leaves and looking for tiger nuts. Mom said, "You'll not find those. They come from a foreign country!"

We told the time with dandelion clocks, blowing the white fluffy seeds into the air and chanting one o'clock two o'clock… Or we counted the points of a prickly holly leaf chanting, 'My mother wants me yes… no… yes… no.' If it ended with 'yes' both times we would laugh and run home, as long as it was close to going home time!

We sat in the green painted sheds on the 'Rec' and if the park-keeper came to chase us out we would call, 'Rhubarb, Rhubarb!' our name for him, and we'd run away laughing!

Sometimes I'd been in the park with Mom and we had seen ladies dressed in long black robes, walking in twos. "Who are they?" I'd asked Mom.

"They're called nuns," she explained, "they live in a convent and they often come to the park, for some fresh air I should think. You can see the convent from here." She pointed into the distance but I could see only trees.

"What do they do there?" I wanted to know.

"They are ladies who are very religious. They shut themselves away from work and pray to God."

"And to Jesus?" My heart was beating fast as I waited for an answer.

"Yes of course! Those nuns you see in the park are allowed out but some orders as they are called, are very strict, and those nuns never leave their convents."

I tried to study the nuns more closely. Only their smooth pink faces were visible under the tight fitting head dresses. Large silver crosses hung round their necks, against their dark robes, and they wore black stockings, with heavy shoes on their feet. I longed to hear them speak. Would one of them mention God or Jesus? Would they be able to show me a picture of Jesus if I asked?

But later, when I went into the park with my school friends I was given a different view of the mysterious ladies.

Clem, Fay's brother said, "They're not like us. They're Catholics! Like the MacNallys."

The MacNally family lived in Bournbrook and were always trouble at school. Fay and I liked Stephen, the youngest boy. He was always nice to us and seemed quite gentle. One day I made the mistake of saying to Clem,

"I like nuns, I do! I like their faces."

He stared at me, "You're barmy you are! Do you know what they do if they catch you? They take you to work in their laundry stripped to the waist, that's what they do! You'd never get out again! My Mom heard that at the shops!"

In that moment any other feelings I'd had for the nuns was replaced by fear, but as I grew older the fascination returned, and a longing to see inside the convent. I wanted to discover the secrets that lay behind those smooth faces, find out what had moved them to shut themselves away from the world and give their lives to God and Jesus.

Dad had said, "They take the easy way out of life." But I was mystified and still fascinated.

I was beginning to like clothes but didn't have many. Mom made me jumpers and pinafores and various aunts 'made over' things for me. The dress in which I'd been photographed on the fur covered box had long gone but I still had the net one from when I was a bridesmaid to one of Godmother's nieces. I'd stood hand-in-hand with Norman, Godmother's son, and I'd felt very embarrassed…

Dad said I was a tomboy and needed sensible clothes, and of course, sensible shoes. I felt very inferior to my friends, especially Fay who possessed those shiny black ankle strap shoes. I had to go to a clinic for foot exercises, and had to have pieces of leather put on the inside edges of all my sensible shoes. I still liked my 'pumps' and I could play in comfort in the yard without making too much noise, if Peter was poorly. How much longer would he live next door? I dreaded the time when he would at last leave for London. I tried to see him as often as I could but Doctor Renwick came more and more to see him. The special teacher had stopped coming.

One day I was sitting in the yard next door. Peter was in his wheelchair and I was on the stool. He looked at me and said, "Do you know, Junie, when I'm lying in bed, sometimes a ray of light comes through the window right on my face! It really warms me up. It's happened a lot lately."

I said hopefully, "Perhaps Jesus is sending some special treatment from heaven. I'm sure he watches over you, Peter." My heart felt heavy for him. He held out his poor bandaged hands to me.

"You are a good girl, Junie. You'll say a prayer for me when I go away won't you?"

I felt tears come to my eyes as I faltered, "I say one every night now, Peter."

"God Bless You, June," he said quietly. He looked at me with his dark-circled brown eyes and I thing we both knew that he had left his childhood behind....

Mom said one day to cheer me up, "You'll soon be able to go to the tuppenny crush on a Saturday but not on your own. Perhaps Fay or Marg will go with you."

I said, "Olive might want to come with us." Mom shook her head. "I don't think her parents would allow that."

I had seen 'Film Fun' magazine so had a taste of the cinema already and I'd heard about various film stars. I looked forward to seeing the inside of the Stirchley Pavilion, we had passed it in the car and it had looked very impressive. Granny Buttercup had often said, "Your Mom is the image of Clara Bow." I'd wondered who this person was and found out that she was a film star!

Marg and I didn't have many hobbies but we did collect orange wrappers which had on them pictures of ladies in mantillas, a kind of lace headdress which Mom explained came from Spain, where the oranges grow. Marg and I found old shoeboxes, cut the ends off and put them on our heads, covered with a teacloth or anything we could find, then we would dance to Mom's record of 'Rio Rita.' My Aunt Doll said she would teach us to play the castanets, whatever they were!

Godmother told us one day that she was going to move house. "It's not far away," she said, "Only in Umberslade Road where the Senior Boys School is. It has a big garden where Gip can run. Now that Norman is going away to school I shouldn't be able to take Gip out three or four times a day, my legs are too bad. You'll like the house and you'll be able to come after school, I'm sure your Mom will bring you." The good news was that Auntie Grace was coming to live in

Godmother's house, just along the passage. I loved my Auntie Grace. She was a year older than Mom, gentle, witty and kind and she often drew pictures of fairies for me when she came to tea. I quite liked my cousin Terry but I have to say that I did not like my Uncle Ernest. There were many reasons for my dislike of him – his intolerance of Auntie's deafness – she was left deaf twenty years earlier through influenza, also, he never took her out, he just went to his local pub every night or played bowls in the park. When I told Mom I hated him she said, "You must never hate anyone," then she added, "Well one good thing, Auntie can come and have a chat round here while he's out playing bowls in the 'Rec'."

I laughed and brightened up, "She's going to show me her dance dress one day." She nodded, "It's lovely. It's green velvet with a spray of lilies of the valley on one shoulder. The shoulders are dropped – very daring."

I laughed then, thinking of Mom's own evening dress which had no back in it as far as the waist!

A few days later Mom said, "Did Mrs Sargent say anything about Peter when you were there the other day?"

I shook my head and she said slowly, "I'm sorry love. I have to tell you. While you were at school today an ambulance came and took Peter and his mother down to London."

I was broken-hearted, "Oh Mom! He was all right. He talked a lot and he didn't bite his fingers at all! I was close to tears and Mom explained, "When someone has to sit all day in a wheelchair various things can go wrong in the body. Peter has to go to a special kidney unit in London." I couldn't believe it had come to this after all! I'd been hoping so much that he would stay. I said brokenly, "Why did Jesus let him be so poorly? He's so good, Mom!"

Mom said, "Jesus can't be everywhere with everybody can he?"

I thought that he could," I said flatly.

Later I cried and said, "I never wished him good luck or goodbye."

"You can send him a letter," she suggested. "I'll write if for you, in a while, I'm sure Mrs Sargent would do the same for Peter. You're very important to him, she knows that, I know it too."

I nodded, "I'll practice my writing."

I didn't want to believe I would never see him again. I enjoyed our talks; I'd made him laugh quite often. When he bit his fingers and I had to leave, I would go and cry in our 'lar' outside.

Some time later I received a letter from Peter, written by his mother. Mr Sargent had found a house to rent, quite near the hospital.

'Everyone is so kind here. You would like the gardens at the hospital. I've seen a red squirrel and there are all kinds of birds, not just your favourite, the sparrow, Junie. I hope you are doing well at school and also at Sunday School. You Dad's bible sounds very interesting. I hope he gives it to you to keep very soon.'

I was delighted to receive the letter and Mom said she would help me with a reply. But I wanted to do one myself. I would feel closer to Peter that way. I was interested to hear about the squirrel. I'd never seen one, only in photographs.

He was right about the sparrow – it would always have a special place in my heart because of the Dell story. However, I was going to have an unpleasant experience in Muntz Park. I'd gone after school one day with Fay and Marg and in the green painted sheds we'd sat and talked, and looked at heart shapes scratched on the woodwork. Fay said how only rough children put swear words but lots of children scratched hearts on, with sets of initials inside them. Then somebody said, "Hey, June Keppy, are you Howard Grey's sweetheart? Your initials are here with his. Look!"

I looked. JK loves HG. I was fuming! I hardly knew the boy! He was older than me too, in another class at school. I'd never spoken to him!

"I'm going to scratch it out!" I shouted and I took a hair grip from my hair. I was in a real rage. Just then the boy, Howard Grey arrived with his friends and somebody showed him the heart. There was a whispered discussion and he came up to me.

"This is for a dare," he said and kissed me on the cheek! Somebody sniggered and I shouted, "Beast Beast!" and hit him across the face as hard as I could! He looked startled and everybody laughed. Then he walked away with his friends. I sat in the shed with my friends, still very angry.

"He asked for it, June," Fay said and Marg nodded.

Several days later something happened. Fay came round to see me and to tell me something horrible.

"They've taken Howard Grey away to the loony bin!"

I was horrified, "Oh no!" Was it my fault? Had my blow to his face anything to do with it? I burst into tears and Fay said, "Don't cry June. He's been going funny for a long time. His Mom told mine."

Just then, Mom came in from shopping. "Whatever's the matter?"

"It's my fault." I sobbed. Fay started to tell her the story in dramatic terms.

"I hit him on the face," I sobbed. Mom tut-tutted. "What is it all about, Fay?" "June?"

I told her about the heart shape and how the boy had kissed my cheek for a dare. She was not smiling.

"How old is this boy?"

"About ten," Fay said. "He's going to the big boys school soon."

Mom sat down and took a deep breath. "Fay, I'm going to say something to June and it applies to you too! Be careful of boys. They grow up quickly. Children turn into adults and they're not always nice. She looked sad for a moment then, "You're both sensible girls. I don't want you to be afraid of growing up but… well… you'll know how to be! Life is more complicated as you grow older. You have to understand that men and women are different from one another."

Fay said, "My Mom says I must never trust men when I grow up."

Mom looked at her seriously, "Well, I wouldn't quite go as far as that but… don't you grow up too quickly. If there's anything either of you want to know about, anything at all, come to me. Keep your childhood as long as you can and always treasure your happiest moments. And if you respect people they will respect you."

Fay left and Mom said, "I can hear your Dad's car. Let's keep this to ourselves. He wouldn't be pleased and he might stop you going to the park."

Dad had come home early as he was taking the band to Wolverhampton that evening. As he sorted out his music I said, "Why is the band called the Emeralds, Dad?"

He smiled at me. "Your Mom chose the name. She said it was from a fairytale. Do you like it?"

"Yes," I said, but I was thinking of that poor boy Howard Gray…

At last I was allowed to go to with Marg and Fay to the tuppenny crush on a Saturday morning. Another school friend, June Livingstone, who had ginger hair, came with us. Her Mom ran a café on the corner of Hubert Road, near to the Baker's shop. We ran down the hill, passed Marg's house, waving to Olive who was watching for us from the front window. At the main road we got someone to take us across and followed the tramlines until we came to the

Pavilion Cinema, a big white building with a curved front, and steps leading up to the front entrance. Crowds of children were already queuing at the side and as soon as the commissionaire opened the doors there was a mad rush. We paid our tuppence and made our way into the stalls. We would have liked to go upstairs but children were not allowed up there on a Saturday morning. The temptation to throw things onto the children below would have been too great! Perhaps some time I would be able to go into the circle with Mom. We managed to get four seats in the middle so that we would have a good view of the screen.

It was a good two pennyworth. There was a cartoon, a film about jungles, then there was an interval and a screen came down and words of songs appeared on it. A man on the seat of a big organ came up from the depths and played music, and we sang songs we had heard at home – 'Roses of Picardy', 'Daisy Bell', 'After the Ball', 'There's a Long Long Trail A-winding.' My one favourite became 'Chapel in the Moonlight' and there was a funny song called 'Wheezy Anna.' The organ disappeared back into the depths, the song screen went up and a serial came on, with Harold Lloyd. It ended with something exciting happening which made us want to come back the following week! We rushed out into the bright sunshine, talking to friends and avoiding the enemies of our school world... Marge left us at her house and Fay, June Livingstone and I carried on up the hill and had a glass of lemonade at our house.

We were never bored in our every day lives. We had hopscotch, whips and tops, marbles and corking, and collecting tram tickets to make concertinas. Everyone in the class had knitted something on four needles, an exciting venture. Mine was a bright orange drawstring bag, with a black tassel at the bottom, and a black cord threaded through the top. I decided to keep my marbles in it and once caused a stir by dropping them all over the classroom!

One day Dad said, "We're going to tea to Aunt Polly's on Sunday, Maggie and Charlie will be there."

I liked Uncle Charlie. He was Aunt Polly's son; a bachelor and he wore strange trousers called Plus Fours. He made his own beer and rolled herbal cigarettes. He was also in the Warwickshire Yeomanry with Dad and they went away sometimes to weekend camp with other ex-service friends of theirs. Polly and Charlie lived in a large Victorian house which was on the Outer Circle bus route in Acocks Green. The house had a lot of interesting things about it, some I liked, and some I didn't. Mom had said that Polly was a walking miracle. She was small and neat, and fifty years ago had been given six months to live but now she was over ninety years old. Maggie was Charlie's second cousin, also unmarried and she ran a shop and café in the centre of Birmingham, where there were factories. Visiting her shop was always exciting and she had promised that when I was older I could go for a day and help serve in the shop. Dad drew the car up onto the small driveway and Polly greeted us. "Maggie's making tea. Come along in my dears."

Charlie appeared and took John's hand, Dad carried Jacqui and Mom and I followed. My heart pounded, for I was about to see something that scared me. In the big hall was a Grandfather clock which ticked so slowly that I always thought that someone was hiding inside! Over the sitting room door was a huge pair of buffalo horns with black fur between them. A dark staircase led up to the bathroom and I hoped that I would not want to 'spend a penny' during the afternoon. Whenever I had been up there before I felt that someone or some… thing… was watching me…

The sitting room was like a museum, with stuffed birds and animals and fish in large glass cases. There were ornate glass shapes under domes, dark oil paintings, several big chairs and a settee. There had always been a pouffé for me but John had found it so I sat on the floor. Maggie greeted us all and handed out cups of tea, lemonade in tall glasses for John and I, and milk for Jacqui which Mom had brought with her. On the mantelpiece was a large gilt clock with cherubs climbing up on each side of it. Polly asked me about school while Charlie and Dad took their tea into the billiard room which led off the hall. I told Maggie what we had been doing at school, so did John. John and Jacqui played together while I listened to the adults talking. The men came back and talked about army horses. Maggie said, "You'll come for a day won't you June, when you're a bit older?"

I nodded eagerly. "Can I weigh things out?"

She smiled. "You can weight the sweets out."

Everyone began talking about something called the League of Nations and I was uneasy. War was looming ever nearer and I could not imagine such a thing. We had a lovely tea and fortunately I didn't have to 'spend a penny' in the white bathroom. As we left Mom said, "Come to us soon Polly," but we all knew she would never come. She rarely went out of the house. Charlie was home on weekdays and Maggie at weekends, when she shut her shop and café.

I was delighted when Mom's younger sister, Aunt Floss, came to live with us. She had a sweet voice, black wavy hair with a 'kiss curl' on her forehead, and hazel eyes like Mom. She had found a job at Selly Oak Hospital which was further along the Raddlebarn Road, so she could come with me as far as Paddy's corner and carry on to the hospital. There was a large house on the opposite side of the road, just past Mr Bonell's bread shop and a nice man who had a limp always stood there in the morning, just waiting to say 'good morning' to Auntie. Mom had hoped that he would pluck up courage to ask her out, but he never did! Eventually she met and married an elderly man called Joe, who had a grown-up family, and went to live at his house in Edgbaston. Two of his daughters were older than Auntie. The youngest, worked for the Post Office and went to a school of dance on Hagley Road. Every Christmas she would do a tap dance for the family at Granny's. She was quite a heavyweight and all the crockery rattled on the Welsh dresser, and everyone giggled. She had a big theatrical basket full of lovely dressing up clothes, made by her real mother, some years earlier. She would never let me try any on but she did produce a pair of block-toed ballet shoes for me to try. As I clomped around the room on my toes, I decided that ballet was definitely not for me!

I was thumbing through one of Uncle Joe's books once on a visit when I came across a word I didn't know.

"What does brothel mean, Uncle?"

This caused a stir! Everyone's face was red, and there was a lot of stammering and stuttering. Uncle Joe said in what must have been panic, "Don't ask silly questions, child!" Then he thought the better of it and added mildly, "It's a place… a place where wicked men and women go."

"Do you mean hell, Uncle?" I wanted to know.

Everyone laughed at that! I wanted the answers to so many questions and never seemed to get them to my satisfaction.

I haunted Selly Oak Library, reading everything I could lay my hands on. It was my haven of peace. 'Silence is Golden' as Mom often said. I loved sitting in the reference section and reading 'Pilgrims Progress.' It was a large black book, bigger the Dad's bible, and there were drawings of the characters met by Christian on his travels. I looked at books in the adult section – Rider Haggard,

Sax Rohmer, H G Wells, Edgar Wallace, though I could not take any out on my Junior ticket. An aunt of Dad's called Jessie Cochrane sent me a copy of 'Ivanhoe' and the 'The Talisman' by Sir Walter Scott, and my as yet unseen Granny in Broadstairs, sent me 'Jane Eyre' which I read three times over! I still didn't know why she and Grandad Beer lived in different towns. Near the library was a bridge, and Marg and I would watch for barges usually laden with coal. Each barge was pulled along the canal by a long rope attached to a horse, which walked on the towpath, with a man alongside. If we were lucky we would see two barges, one going one way, one the other.

Dad bought me a book called 'The English Landscape in Prose and Poetry' which had photographs as well as words. He gave me his two volumes of Shakespeare's plays; I read the set of Dickens, and the Life Story of Napoleon. Books became my life. I had realised that sitting in the 'lar' counting bricks on the wall was not the way to improve my mind! Marg and I often went to Woolworth's 3d 6d store and we discovered little books of line drawings at sixpence each. They showed all sorts of subjects, armour, costumes, castles, furniture and other things. When I told Dad about the books he took me to the store and bought me three. I'd never seen anything like them before.

I'd joined the Band of Hope which met at a hall on Raddlebarn Road where Sunday school was also held. I was given a triangle to play in the band and we sang 'Death to Alcohol' and 'Members of the White Ribbon Band.' The meetings were presided over by Miss Sturge, a prim little lady who wore a pince-nez on her nose. At the touch of a button the pince-nez jumped off her nose, onto her dress and up to the button. Fascinating!

I had one of my wishes. We had begun going to Lickey Hills, Birmingham's own beauty spot. We waited for the tram which had an open end on the top deck, scrambling up to the long polished seat so that we could hang on, giggling our way to the terminus. Near the Rednal terminus was a green painted tearoom called Bilberry Tea Room and we could take our own sandwiches and buy a glass of pop, watching the fairground from the window. We didn't often have enough money to go on any of the rides but were just content to watch. There was a lovely custardy ice cream made by a company called York Jones and as we licked our cornets we climbed the shallow steps towards the summit of the nearest hill. We roamed in the woods where the bluebells made a magic carpet amongst tall, straight trees. We scuffed our feet amongst dead leaves from the previous year and the scent of the bluebells assailed the senses. We picked armfuls to take home and they soon dropped, but once we were home they revived in a vase of water but not for long.

As a treat Dad took John and myself to New Street Station which had an entrance at the front in Stephenson Place and one at the back near the markets. A continuous wind blew right through and the smell of the trains was like no other. Each platform was reached through an arch at the top of a flight of steps and sometimes Dad would buy a platform ticket and take us down.

"We'll go on a train one of these days," he would say, but it would be a few years before I got my wish.

In the Bull Ring gypsies stood with baskets of cowslips for sale at tuppence a bunch. There was a statue of Lord Nelson and it was here that speakers stood and talked of politics and religion. The Market Hall was a delight. Above the entrance was a clock, with paired figures striking bells with hammers. Inside were all kinds of shops, including pet shops where we looked at puppies, kittens and rabbits.

Life had a regular pattern, happy and secure, apart from missing Peter more than I could say. I hadn't received a letter for some weeks and was feeling unaccountably sad.

Coming home from school one day I looked at Mom's face and knew that she had some bad news. In a strange way I was prepared – a few nights earlier I'd seen Peter's face in my room and I'd felt very cold…

She said gently, "I'm so sorry, June."

"Peter has died hasn't he?" It didn't sound like my voice speaking the words. She took my hand,

"It was for the best, love. Better now than sitting for years and years in his chair, growing into a man."

I drew a deep breath, my heart pounding.

"Why did Jesus let him die, he was so good Peter was. He never swore or spat or threw stones like other boys."

She frowned at me. "Is that what's happened to you at school? You've never said."

I shook my head and looked down at my hands because my eyes were full of tears. The red marks had long gone but the memory of my first day at Infants' school would always be with me.

I said then, "Can I write to Mr and Mrs Sargent and tell them how I am?"

"Come and sit down," she led me to a chair in the sitting room, "and I'll try and explain about his illness."

"He was born with what is called an abnormality of the brain. Something growing in his head and biting his fingers was part of the illness."

I stared at her. "He was so clever, Mom! He made me laugh and he listened to me, not like Clem!"

My voice broke and she said, "I'll help you write the letter in a little while."

I sat for a long time while Mom prepared tea. I had not had a chance to say goodbye to my sweetheart. I tried to imagine him singing our song 'If I Had a Talking Picture' and I wanted to believe that we would meet again some day...

As I grew older time stopped flying by and life seemed to become more serious. I was soon in trouble with the Headmistress of the Junior School. Miss Forrest, my teacher, said I was not paying attention in class and she sent me to the Head, Miss Coslett. I stood in the dark corridor outside her room waiting for my punishment which I'd heard would be a smack with a ruler...

I could hear a quarrel going on inside the room.

"I will not put up with flirting in this school! You should be ashamed of yourselves behaving like that in front of children!"

I was all agog to see who the teachers were and when the door opened Miss Parker, the girls' gym teacher and Mr Dean, the boys' gym teacher came out with red faces. Soon afterwards they left the school and got married!

I'd never been sporty but when Uncle Jack gave me his old tennis racquet I was delighted. Mom said, "It's a nice racquet but you won't be able to play on the courts in the Rec yet a-while." We could see the courts from our house and one day I hoped to play on them with my friends. We had to be fourteen years old.

I'd told Auntie Grace that I'd seen Peter's face in our kitchen and she looked scared. Mom frowned, "You shouldn't have told her. She gets frightened about things like that. She's very timid."

Mom believed in ghosts and had seen one or two, she told me. She didn't mind talking about people who had passed away because she believed they were not gone forever but waiting in heaven for their loved ones. That gave me quite a bit of comfort. Peter had looked happy and well and we would meet again, I was sure...

Every year a carnival took place in Selly Oak Park and as Marg and I paid our tuppence we knew that this would be our last. We were getting too grown up to walk in with a cup on a string round our necks! We received our white paper bag containing a bun and a 'surprise'. Marg and I both received a hankie with pictures on them. There were the usual jazz bands and sideshows and the previous year a man had chased us because we had seen him putting a false nose on a dog, then putting up a sign which said 'See the Rat as Big as a Dog!

An era was coming to an end for all of us who had attended Raddlebarn Road Infants' and Juniors' School...

Journeys alone by tram car into Birmingham centre and beyond meant that I'd reached another turning point in my happy, sheltered life of family, friends, Infants' and Junior Schools.

There had been feelings of success, moments of pride in Mom and Dad's approval of school reports, teachers' high hopes of those pupils including myself, who had sat their entrance exams for Secondary, Grammar or High Schools. I knew I was not clever enough to aspire to King Edwards High and chose instead Kings Norton Secondary School, an all girls' school. As I'd sat in a strange classroom I'd known I would not be happy. I suppose deep down I knew that achieving success in the future was going to be more of an effort than it had been at Junior School. Dorothy Sanderson, my desk companion in the Infants' School, had moved house and chose George Dixon Grammar School in Edgbaston. We had promised to keep in touch with one another.

My childhood friends Fay and Marg were moving to the 'awful' school as Dad had once called it, quite unfairly I'm sure. Fay was expected to help her Dad run the garage office and Marg, dear, uncomplaining Marg would continue to look after her handicapped sister Olive as their parents were ailing fast.

Dad had been to see another house off the Bristol Road. It was semi-detached, with a built-in garage for Dad's car and to our delight, a bathroom and indoor toilet. The house lay back from an expanse of grass and beyond was the road itself, Weoley Park Road, lined with Beech trees, and fairly free of traffic. It would be a five-minute walk to Selly Oak to catch the number eleven Outer Circle bus to my new school.

I missed my friends very much; I missed the 'Rec', the shops, and above all Muntz Park. I'd finally achieved my ambition and seen the Dell at close quarters on several summer evenings with Mom and Auntie Grace when there was a dance going on. I'd looked in vain for the special place where the sparrow of Mom's story had stood on its tiny legs to go down into fairyland. But the fantasy was over – I had no feelings of betrayal about being told such stories in my childhood. It had been necessary to have a period of make believe – the world would all too quickly become reality to a growing child…

I left years of childhood with a growing awareness, a little fearful. I had to be self-reliant from now on. No longer could I look to my parents for comforts and have decisions made for me.

Although I'd left Raddlebarn Road Junior School with a good report, and the hopes of teachers pinned on many of us, I felt suddenly very vulnerable. No longer would I have Paddy the policeman, my friends, Fay and Marg, the park with the Dell, for we were moving house.

I would miss Mr Powell's corner shop, with its musty smell, the sacks of rice, sugar and flour, the tubs of butter, the sides of bacon. I would miss the tangy smell of cheese and with rind, and miss seeing pickles in jars.

I didn't want to leave my cosy, if sometimes violent schooldays, nor the house with its small garden, the brick entry that took my voice and threw it so eerily. I would miss the outside 'lar' where I'd sat on the wooden seat at odd times of day, counting the bricks on the walls and pretending to be Queen Mary. I would miss playing on the tyres with Fay and Clem, going to the tuppenny crush on a Saturday morning, seeing Gip, my Godmother's lovely dog who knew me so well.

I would miss so many things… and I still missed Peter.

Signs of war loomed on the horizon and the Baldwin government issued leaflets on air raid precautions, sending an unfamiliar shaft of apprehension through us all. Dad had said that the war he'd fought in had been the war to end all wars. There had been no real victory, he'd said, no real prosperity for ordinary men who, with feelings of guilt over their own survival thought so often of their dead comrades. Dad was very much involved with ex-servicemen and spent much of his time working for them through his club. He was a self-made man, a born organiser. He still had his dance bands and now a military band. He still organised Poppy Day and other flag days for Birmingham and I was allowed with my new friend Betty Small to sell flags or poppies in cinema foyers or city arcades. We were too young to sell them on the street. It was quite an adventure for us. People were always very kind and there was always a drink of pop for us, and the excitement of finding out how much money we had collected in our tins.

The Warriors Club was thriving and the magazine 'The Warrior' was warning of the growth of Nazism, and the folly of disarmament. I couldn't bear the thought of Dad or any of my uncles having to go and fight in a war. The few visits to Thorp Street Drill Hall that I made with Dad where he had his Poppy Day office would stay with me forever and I began to understand the futility of war and the dreadful aftermath. Now I needed more than a likeness to Jesus to help me cope with the coming years and yet ... the quest was still there at the back of my mind...

I was eleven years old and had begun my time at Kings Norton Secondary School. From day one I disliked every subject except French and Latin. Inexplicably I disliked particularly English Grammar, to which I should have paid more than a little attention. I'd enjoyed Composition at Junior School and had expected my enthusiasm to develop. Inspired by a cut out model of a huntsman riding a horse which stood on our mantelpiece I wrote my first poem called 'The Hunt.' It was pulled to pieces and ridiculed in front of the class, and subsequently my creative urges I might have had were then driven into my subconscious.

It's strange though, how sentences linger in the mind – 'Methought I heard a voice cry sleep no more, Macbeth does murder sleep, the innocent sleep, sleep that knits up the ravelled sleeve of care, the death of each day's life, sore labour's bath, balm of hurt of minds...' Sleep was no balm to me in my early years. I had bad dreams, had seen shadows on walls despite the disappearance of gas mantles – we had electricity in our new home. I lived in a different world to my contemporaries: fears and obsessions abounded yet I'd had a happy secure and interesting childhood, fulfilled, loving and innocent, as every child's life should be. And yet those early years had been filled with that longing to see a likeness of our Lord. It was still there...

P.T. lessons were a disaster to me at Kings Norton Secondary School. Invariably I was dragged half-fainting from the gymnasium, I was hopeless at netball, hockey and swimming. I was bottom, almost in every subject except French and Latin. Mom had said, to cheer me up, "You've got your very own talents to see you through life. Things have a way of working out, June."

We had no biology lessons, no hygiene education. When a girl named Doreen Mason came to me one day and whispered 'Are you one of the seven?' I thought she meant a secret girls' club! I didn't even know that she meant seven girls who had started their monthly periods! Even had mistakenly thought that we had been told at school about what came to be known as 'the curse', and the facts of life. We all believed that if a man kissed you it would cause pregnancy and that a baby was born through the navel! Such innocence we had in those days, with no urgent inclination to find out the truth!

By the end of 1938 I'd become depressed and unhappy. The daily bus journey through Bournville became a chore.

Preparations for war moved relentlessly forward. An air raid warden service was created and the Women's Volunteer Service was formed. Anderson shelters for gardens and Morrison shelters for indoors were made available to the public but for some reason Dad had refused, saying that would take away our chance at the nearest public shelter being dug out that very moment half a mile away on Shenley Fields Road. I knew I would have a problem for I hated being cooped up, hated going underground.

Mom and Dad didn't talk much about war in front of me unless Uncle Charlie or other friends came to the house, then the conversation became uninhibited and intense. Men's talk of war was so different from that of the women…

During the last school holiday I would have whilst attending Kings Norton School Dad put me on a train to Broadstairs to meet for the first time his mother, Granny Camille. I'd heard a great deal about her over the years, how she had married at 16, given birth to Jack, Dad's eldest brother at 17, how Grandad 'Beer' as I called him, treated her badly when he was 'in drink' and how she escaped by climbing down a rope of knotted sheets from her bedroom. She took with her the youngest boy, Fred, and was heavily pregnant with a daughter to be called Winnie. She sought refuge with her sister Kitty in London and together they set up a hotel business in Bournemouth. Dad and Jack had been left in the clutches of a cruel housekeeper who was supposed to be taking care of the boys. The boys left home as soon as they could, Uncle Jack joining the Royal Navy and Dad went to Australia and other places.

Granny Camille met me at Broadstairs Station, a tiny figure with a bright birdlike face and a loud voice with a Welsh accent. I was intrigued because I had known no other accent but 'Brummagem.' She kissed me, looked at my navy school blazer and cotton check dress and took me into a shop where she bought me two floral dresses and a pair of sensible shoes. I was soon to discover that a great part of my holiday would be spent in preparing vegetables for the guests in her hotel. After finishing my chores I was free to please myself so after lunch each day I went to the beautiful beach where 'Uncle Mac's Minstrel Show' took place and it was free. At night the show moved to the jetty but there was an entrance fee so I stood at the back listening to the music. Mom and Dad had given me half a crown each and I felt quite rich. Granny Camille said I must get back at the hotel by nine o'clock each night and one night a ginger-haired boy followed me back. I sent him packing. I was not yet interested in male company!

Granny spent much of her spare time with Auntie Gwen who was Uncle Fred's wife. They too had a hotel in the town. It was amazing how much like Dad she was, in looks but not personality.

She said before I returned to Birmingham, "I wouldn't have left your Dad and Uncle if I'd known how the housekeeper would treat them."

I said defensively, "Oh, they managed all right! Uncle Jack joined the navy and Dad became a soldier after he'd been to Australia!" I did thank her, however, for the copy of 'Jane Eyre' she'd sent me a few years earlier.

I'd enjoyed Broadstairs but once I was back home I decided to try and force the issue, persuade Dad to let me leave Kings Norton before School Certificate. I couldn't face the thought of more months or years at the school. I wanted to go out in the real world and work – work at anything. The snag was that Dad would have to pay a £5 penalty if I left early. It was a lot of money. His business was being affected by the threat of war. But I worked on him long and hard. Then one day, out of the blue he said, "All right, you can leave. I'll find the five pounds but I'll get you a job myself then I'll know where you are. You're still only fifteen, remember."

I was overjoyed and wondered secretly if Mom had influenced his decision. She had known how unhappy I'd been. The weeks began to fly and suddenly it was the last day at the school. I took my autograph book with me to get the signatures of my two favourite teachers, Miss Robertson who taught Latin and Miss Hancock who taught French, and some of my friends in Form 5A.

I was free at last but I had to admit I would miss hearing the bells playing 'Vicar of Bray' as the bus went through Bournville. I would miss seeing the green covered with crocuses in spring too, but at home I would still smell the cocoa when rain was imminent. A strange phenomenon, which affected the area, but a pleasant one.

The last peacetime outing which Dad would organise for his beloved ex-servicemen was a trip by train to the Aldershot Tattoo. Mom and I went too and enjoyed it very much but on the way home my neck began to hurt - I had developed mumps! At home we found that my sister Jacqui, who was being looked after by Uncle Frank and Aunt Jess had also developed it! Dad bought us a bunch of black grapes each and when I felt better he said, "I'll show you a map of Europe then you'll understand what is happening."

Chamberlain had been to Munich to sign the peace pact but Dad said, "Nothing will stop Hitler. He's already grabbed Czechoslovakia."

I asked, "Is that near Moravia?"

"Moravia? Where did you hear that?"

Mom explained to Dad, "There's a brother and sister at the college - the boy, Ernst, told June that they wanted to go back home."

He said slowly, "They would do better to stay here. Are they Jews?"

Mom didn't know and he said, "They would be interned if they stayed here," and explained the significance of internment.

The ARP Services had been mobilised and we were issued with gas masks. War was coming uncomfortably close. I couldn't associate God with war yet Dad told me that strange things happened in the 1914–18 one. He told that a vision known as the 'Angel of Mons' had appeared to both sides, and yet they continued to fight one another. There was no sense in it at all.

The Secondary School had dominated my life for the past three years and now I would be starting a job, a real job with a salary of eighteen shillings a week. There was a lot of activity in the city centre, with increasing numbers of servicemen crowding into the railway stations, Snow Hill and New Street Stations. Barrage balloons appeared round the city skies like alien space craft. At first they were regarded with amusement until we learned that their purpose was to deter German dive-bombers. In St Philip's Cathedral churchyard, one lunchtime, an army band came to play in the bandstand. A tall young soldier in dress uniform sang 'One Alone' from 'Desert Song' and I suddenly felt very sad that everyone's lives were about to change. Mine had changed along since, with dear Peter, Fay and Marg, and the others a fast disappearing memory, a memory being pushed out by the seriousness of the situation.

Dad had taken me to Birmingham Town Hall to hear the Prime Minister make a speech. There had been a commotion at the back of the hall and people had been hustled out by police. We sat in the front row and he seemed to fix me with a cold gaze. Perhaps it was a politician's trick or perhaps I represented something unfamiliar to him – youth, the youth of a country about to be sacrificed as it had in 1914.

Piles of sandbags began to appear outside public buildings and strips of sticky tape were placed criss-cross on large windows to minimise bomb blast...

At family gatherings the men talked of war but the women sat looking at one another with unspoken dread. Mom had been so kind, tolerant and patient, so long-suffering of Dad's absences from the house with his dance bands, his Warrior Club meetings, the flag days, soon to vanish for the duration.

By September 1938 3½ million people had been evacuated from cities, mainly school children and mothers with children under five. My brother and sister would soon be leaving home too. We had heard that there was now total blackout in London and Mom decided to make her own blackout curtains for our house – it was inevitable that Birmingham would be targeted as well as other large industrial cities. Birmingham was England's second city in every way. Petrol was rationed and pooled, at one and six a gallon so we wouldn't be able to use the car much.

However, Dad had arranged for Mom to go on a cruise to Madeira and Lisbon. It was something that she had never thought would happen so Dad had thought 'now or never.' I had misgivings about her going alone but Dad had commitments and the three of us to think about. We all set off for Liverpool where the P & O liner S.S. Montclare was berthed. I had never seen such a sight. She was beautiful. We were able to see some of the salons and marvelled at the cost of them – £14 for 15 days. With a few minor disasters I cooked the meals and we were very relieved when we received a postcard from Madeira. Mom was enjoying herself and looking forward to going on to Lisbon. However, in the middle of the night, on August 30th, the ship was blacked out and returned with all speed to Liverpool. Dad made the journey by train to collect her and later had a rebate of £4! The S.S. Montclare and her sister ships the 'Montrose' and 'Moncalm' became troop ships, sadly to be lost to enemy action.

Mom bought me two blouses and a skirt for my new job, as I didn't have many clothes. Dad got me a job as a Hollerith operator at Stewart's and Lloyd's in Easy Row, off Paradise Street in the city. A friend of his was a Buyer there. I would be earning a real salary so there may be a few shillings left for clothes after I'd given Mom my 'keep.' No one had yet seen nylon stockings and we didn't expect to see them in England for many years. Dad bought all the newspapers, avidly watching developments as everyone was. One day he came home with a second-hand radio, in a wooden cabinet on legs. He and Mom were going out that night and he warned me 'don't touch anything.' But I found a wire at the back where it said 'aerial' and put it up on the picture rail. Twiddling the knobs I heard Henry Hall and his Orchestra from Berlin! It was so thrilling. When Mom and Dad came home they forgave my curiosity and Dad tried it himself. Then we heard the voice of Adolf Hitler. We had never heard anything like it before. Dad said, "He's a madman."

On September 1st Germany invaded Poland and the die was cast. Blackout was already in force all over the country and official evacuation continued. My brother John was sent to Gloucester and my sister Jacqui to Wythall just outside Birmingham. I was delighted to be staying at home but at the back of my mind I knew that if the war lasted many years I would be called up. I couldn't see the sense in war – young innocent men being sent to kill others like themselves, all because of the inadequacy of politicians, and their failure to keep peace with one another. But Hitler, it seemed, was power drunk. Dad said, "He's got to be stopped and that means Britain, but Nazism is all over Germany. The man's very popular."

Dad tied up loose ends of business ventures and put away a lot of his music. War was coming and everything would change. We had moved to another house, in Weoley Hill but it was rented. Mom loved it because there was a lean-to greenhouse attached to the garage, and a lovely garden with apple trees.

Dad, unpredictably, had bought a little puppy on the morning of September 3rd 1939. Mom and Dad, the puppy and myself walked along Witherford Way to look at the public air raid shelter in Shenley Fields Road which was now finished. Dad said we should use it as a rendezvous, wherever any of us had been during a raid. About fifty yards from home the puppy stopped, looked up at Dad, his fur standing on end. Then he jerked the lead out of my hand and ran back the way we had come. Had he seen something not of this world, some tragedy known only to God?

"I'll go and shut him in the house," I said and set off. Mom called, "Give him a drink, June, then catch us up."

At the shelter I looked at the entrance and said, "I'm not going down there, Dad. I don't like being shut in anywhere."

He frowned at me, "Young lady, it will be more dangerous to stand up top. There'll be shrapnel falling as well as bombs."

Back home Mom made tea and Dad switched on the radio. It was eleven o'clock. The mournful voice of Neville Chamberlain filled the room. Britain was at war with Germany.

I felt as if some giant hand had come down on us all and I thought, 'Thank heaven Dad is too old to be a soldier again." He was actually forty-three years old at the time.

Life up 'til that moment had been secure and happy, but after the Prime Minister's speech there had been silence in the room.

Dad did not follow his usual routine of putting on the gramophone after lunch but sat for a long time staring into space. He had marvelled at his own survival in the last war - 'I heard it coming - the shell with my name on it. It landed right next to me and didn't explode!' He had told the story so many times with such wonderment. Now perhaps he was wondering if he would survive the coming war. Perhaps the little puppy did sense something. Sadly we had to take him back to the kennels as we would all be out of the house every day, and probably every night from now on.

I was thankful to be starting work - at least for the moment I wouldn't be separated from Mom and Dad.

My sweetheart, Peter, had died in hospital far away from Birmingham, so I'd been spared the agony of seeing his life slip away after his short lifetime of pain. One of my few Secondary School friends, Jean Malkin, had been killed the previous summer. She had fallen under a bus from her cycle, and whenever I thought of her I could feel her pain physically, the way I'd felt the pain of Christ's crucifixion, when I was a child. Mom had said I would always be a deep thinker.

Although Mom was my anchor, Dad dominated the household, bringing reality and discipline into my somewhat day-dreamy life. For years I'd feared his temper and his impatience, and recognised an intellect too great for his environment. There had been flashes of warmth and love though, we were father and daughter and he expected great things of me, and also of my brother

John who was four years younger than I was. From Mom I had learned patience, wisdom, tolerance and economy. I didn't know at the time how little income there was which Mom had to use wisely. She had known poverty in her childhood and yet there was an unbreakable bond in her family. Those members of it who had already passed away were as alive through Mom's belief in the hereafter as they had been when I stayed in the humble house in Argyle Street as a child.

I'd begun my first job at a momentous time – Monday September 4th, 1939. Our boss, Miss Price and her deputy Miss Shaw were the opposite of some of the teachers I'd known recently. They were kind, considerate and broad-minded, and they made up for much of the unhappiness I'd had at the Secondary School.

There were nine girls in the large office on the fourth floor. Two were engaged to soldiers and one, Lucy, was married to an RAF boy who had already gone abroad. We sat in rows of three punching information from invoices onto Hollerith cards which were then fed into a large sorting machine, operated by a senior girl at the front of the room. We all got along very well and those of us who were unattached became very concerned for the others whose men folk were now on active service.

An exciting event took place during my second year in the job. A War Weapons week was held to raise money for a warship and the troops assembled in the West End Cinema car park at the back of our office block. Some cinemas had closed for a while at least. The vast open space suddenly filled with vehicles and armoured cars, all tended with pride by young, bright-faced men in battledress, so innocent and untried. Little did we know how ill prepared Britain was for war. Disarmament had been relentlessly carried out in the thirties despite warnings from ex-servicemen like my Dad, then we began to re-arm too late. The young soldiers on seeing girls looking down at them from the windows tried to woo in an unconventional manner! Each put his name and place of hopeful assignation and time on a piece of paper, wrapped it round a stone and threw it up to the lady of his choice. The bosses on each floor turned a blind eye to the wooing, no doubt in sympathy with the young people. To many of us at first the war was an adventure rather than a danger, the 'phoney war,' as it was being called in the beginning, but by early 1940 we were having more daily air raid warnings in

Birmingham. Each morning, by ten o'clock the warning sounded and we went down to the basement, taking our knitting with us, trying to ignore what might be going on above ground. Then on the all clear we returned to our work. Some of us were knitting a certain 'Woman' magazine bubble pattern jumper in 'Morning Mist' wool, mysteriously coupon-free at that time bought from Birmingham's poshest store, Marshal & Snelgrove, in New Street, later to be bombed.

We had also discovered with great delight cards of pure white cotton at tuppence a card, also coupon-free, from Denleys, a famous button shop in Coronation Street. Knitted double it made a lovely summer jumper for a few shillings.

As the Battle of Britain grew in intensity, we girls gave up collecting film stars' pictures and collected instead pictures of air aces like Guy Gibson, Douglas Bader, Sailor Malan, Paddy Finucane, Cats-Eyes Cunningham and others. Sadly, so many of them died within weeks.

In the canteen we ate our lunch and listened to the one o'clock news read by BBC newsreaders like Alvar Liddell, Bruce Belfrage, Frank Phillips and Wilfred Pickles. As they reported the battles taking place in the skies over the south of England we cheered German losses, shed tears over our own, knowing in our hearts that the death of every young man, enemy or friend, was a tragedy. Youth was fighting the war physically but the older generations bore the agony of it all and their mature shoulders proved far from frail.

There were some daylight raids in the city but the night raids became very intense. By seven o'clock each evening dogs howled, seconds before the siren sounded its eerie warning, chilling the blood. Then came the deep throbbing of heavily laden German bombers. Searchlights were switched on, piercing the sky and the anti-aircraft guns began firing. As Dad had predicted, shrapnel would fall and later there were sites with rockets, in fields, some not far from our home, firing in quick succession, cracking the ears.

After every raid transport was disrupted, the remains of bombed buildings blocking the roads, tramlines twisted, craters appearing. It was usual for those of us who worked in the city centre to travel by tram as far as Pebble Mill Road. There we would get off and walk the rest of the way into town, or hitch a lift en masse in lorries, wondering if our own particular office block would still be there after the night's raid.

In August the Royal Air Force carried out their first raid on Berlin and this boosted morale. In a mounting fever we worked and knitted and cheered and cried yet it seemed strangely unreal. But gradually, as the daily lists of casualties grew thicker on notice boards the horror of the raids began to dawn. Most evenings Betty and I danced at a local church hall 'hop', entrance one penny, run by the vicar, Pastor Smith. It was mainly for the benefit of soldiers billeted in the nearby King Edwards School on Bristol Road. At the height of an air raid he would regretfully close up, and Betty and I would dodge policemen and air raid wardens in an effort to reach the shelter in Shenley Fields Road where we all met. Sometimes Dad and I would stand and watch the searchlights but he had been right about the danger of shrapnel – it came down like deadly rain – we were safer in the shelter.

In November the city of Coventry was bombed, the cathedral devastated and there were many casualties. Birmingham was still suffering greatly of course.

Mom was working shifts at Hollymoor Hospital in Northfield and it was continually filling with wounded men of all nationalities. I had begun visiting one of the wards, talking to men whose families couldn't travel to see them. Many of them were from Scottish regiments.

My brother John became very unhappy in Gloucester. His so-called foster mother took great delight in telling him regularly that Birmingham had been flattened. He wrote to Dad in desperation saying that he was going to run away, so Dad, Mom and I went to collect him. He stayed at home for a little while and we gave him reassurance and comfort, but the law was the law and he had to be evacuated again. This time he was sent to Loughborough where he attended Grammar school. My sister Jacqui was quite happy in Wythall.

Dad's office was bombed; the building, Quadrant Chambers was on the corner of Worcester Street, which led to the Bull Ring. Whilst Mom, Dad and I sorted through the rubble my aunt Doll arrived, as white as a sheet. She told us the awful news that Aunt Jess, wife of Uncle Frank had been killed in a neighbour's garden shelter the previous night. Mom said, "I must go to Frank," and she left with Aunt Doll. Aunt Jess had been such a lovely person, with a lovely singing voice. Her favourite, which she often sang to me as a child was 'Chiribiribin' from one of the shows.

One of the events still talked about at great length at Hollymoor was the evacuation of Dunkirk. The sea had been rough and stormy for weeks beforehand and then as the evacuation began it calmed. Many of the men said it had been a miracle. Nevertheless it had left a great wound in the pride of the nation but we all knew that one day our army would return to France. We were fighting Germany alone. France had fallen and America was keeping out as long as possible. The Channel Islands were now occupied by the Germans and Dad was worried about a family he used to stay with. He had heard that the daughters had been sent to work in Germany but we never did hear the truth.

Many of the intake at Hollymoor were from the Middle Eastern theatre of war and the hospital were asking for volunteers to visit some of the French and colonial servicemen who had found themselves at the hospital. Mom had mentioned the I had learned French at Kings Norton so I was soon recruited. It would be good practice for me but I was finding it fairly difficult to cope with fast moving conversations with excitable patients! They all seemed delighted to hear something that resembled their mother tongue and one group of colonials presented me with a large white bag on their departure. Embarrassed, I opened it and found that they had been saving all their sweet rations for me!

At four o'clock on a Saturday afternoon when I made my visit the bell would ring and Matron would tour the wards to make sure all visitors had gone. I sat on the piano stool in the day room of Sister Jones' ward surrounded by patients who hid me until Matron had been and gone. We would then have an extra chat and Sister Jones would then give me tea and fruitcake in her office. She never seemed to mind the rule breaking as long as her 'dear boys' were happy. I wrote to two of the Free French pilots to improve my French but they went abroad again and put so many place-names in their letters to me that the censor cut them to pieces. There was very little left for me to learn by!

The sight of wounded men was very upsetting but there were some happy times for them. At a Christmas party Evelyn Laye, the musical comedy star came to sing. She was dressed in a long white gown, with a red and blue sash at the waist. There were all kinds of concerts laid on, and a chaotic version of musical chairs in the long hall, dancing to a very good service band. Outside if the weather was kind, patients played football in their pyjamas and dressing gowns in the long grass.

I felt I should be doing more towards the war effort but I was still only sixteen.

On December 30th 1940 Dad went to bed with pains in his legs, and a headache. He had never been ill in his life, he told us, apart from being wounded in the last war. This we only found out by accident from a notebook we found much later. On December 31st he went into a coma and was taken to Selly Oak hospital. About 6.30 the next evening the telephone rang. I answered it and the ward sister said, "Will you ask Mrs Keppy to come. Mr Keppy is not so well." But Mom, sitting in the other room had felt cold hands close over hers a few moments earlier and she knew he had passed away. The vicar for some reason would not let me go to the Chapel of Rest but I did go to the funeral. It was a Masonic funeral. The organ played 'On Wings of Song', the grave was lined with artificial grass and mimosa was sprinkled on the coffin. Despite the cold day I felt a warm glow through my body and after the service the vicar came and said 'God Bless you, child', I never knew why.

Mom, of course, believed in the hereafter, and we began to go to spiritualist meetings. Although I was somewhat sceptical I enjoyed them. There was no table tapping, dimmed lights or gimmickry, just a long drab room lined with chairs and bare wooden floor. Middle-aged and elderly widows with tired gentle faces were all seeking proof of the immortality of their loved ones. Mom, at thirty-nine, was the youngest of them.

One night I received with great delight a message just for me. Mrs Hughes, the jolly white-haired medium said, "I can see a dog here. He's big. I think he's an Airedale; he has brown wiry fur. He's come to you and his name is Gip."

I could scarcely believe it. My thoughts flew back to my childhood, at the house in Wardwards Lane, Godmother Plimmer and our beloved Gip. Mrs Hughes had never met us before, knew nothing about us.

I always hoped to receive a message from Peter but I never did.

Dad's sudden death from meningitis didn't hit us for a while; such was the intensity of the war. There was no time for anyone to stop and grieve properly for their loved ones. Miss Price at the office was very kind and understanding whenever I had a cry. Then a friend of Dad's rang Mom and asked her if I would like to go and work for him. He was Branch Manager of an Insurance Office in Birmingham. I didn't really want to leave Stewart's and Lloyd's but Mom thought if was a good idea, so to please her I went. He was a lovely gentle man but the job was spoiled for me by the Secretary. Each morning I would arrive for work and she would sit me down and take out a comb. She would then proceed to comb my curly hair right back behind my ears to make me look as plain as possible. She began to find fault with everything I did until after three months I felt very unhappy and ready to leave. But I didn't want to offend the Colonel, as we knew him. Then something terrible happened. HMS Hood was sunk by the Germans and his only son was killed. I arrive at the office and saw him sitting at his desk in tears. I had never in my life seen a man cry. Later I did give notice though I felt guilty but apart from an unhappy relationship with the Secretary circumstances had changed. Money was short, Mom received no widow's pension and had only her hospital salary to keep with the little I was giving her – my salary was still not high. I knew I must find a job nearer home to save on fares and be closer so that I could be home to prepare our meal and do the shopping better than I was doing. Then I had some luck. In Weoley Park Road was the Middlemoor Emigration Home, the children long-gone to the Colonies. The building was requisitioned by the Government and the Austin Company took it over as offices for they had a 'shadow' factory in Longbridge. I went to the local labour office and applied for a job there. I had spent three months at the Colonel's office and I still missed the girls at Stewart's and Lloyd's. We had promised to keep in touch. I got a job as a cost clerk at Austin; the large assembly hall had been made into one large office, with others on the upper floor. I no longer had fares to find into Birmingham so it did save me a little money.

On May 10th 1941 London had its last and worst air raid and morale was at an all time low. The men in our offices were being gradually conscripted and some of the girls began applying for release from the company. By June of that year 60,000 women were in the forces and I began to wonder how long it would be before I would be called up. Clothes, cheese, eggs and jam were now rationed. Two million homes had been destroyed in the bombing, 60 per cent in London alone. Birmingham, Britain's second city had really suffered at the hands of the enemy.

None of us could imagine what the end would be. Germany had invaded Russia and the feeling was that this might help us in the long run. It was a great relief to everyone that Hitler had made such a mistake.

By the end of 1941 there was full conscription for unmarried women; 20–30 year old women were subject to call up either for munitions work or the services. I was seventeen now and I wanted to do more. On December 6th the

Japanese attacked Pearl Harbour whilst their minister was talking 'peace.' America was at last in the war.

Vitamins in the form of cod liver oil, rosehip syrup and orange juice were introduced for children and expectant mothers, and blood donors were urgently called for. When a mobile blood donor van came to our offices everyone queued up to give their blood. I was humiliated to be told that I was anaemic and the doctor in charge sent me back to my desk with two packets of iron pills. I was very upset, more determined than ever to do more but it might be difficult to obtain release from the company. Only two other girls had so far managed to obtain it.

January 1942 brought the American forces to Britain and not surprisingly they targeted the British girls, many of whom would end up as GI Brides. They seemed to be everywhere, lounging against tombstones in St Philip's Churchyard, endlessly chewing their gum. They were well dressed and well paid and had plenty of confidence but my opinion was that there were none braver than our brave and honourable British soldiers and airmen.

There was very little petrol now for private use and for a time a kind of gasbag appeared on top of some of the cars. The clothes ration was cut again and more food was rationed including rice and dried fruit.

By May 1942 Singapore had fallen and there were many more restrictions. We already had identity cards, and Mom and I had great fun trying to measure five inches of water into the bath.

Dad's Aunt in South Africa began sending us tins of sausage meat, crayfish and pecan nuts, all very welcome as addition to our diet… Food was generally of good quality, even the sausage and corned beef were tasty.

The latest contingent of wounded at Hollymoor were very depressed. Most of them had been in the Middle East where there had been no victory for us as yet. The Germans were threatening Cairo and Alexandria. Then in October came victory at El Alamein and some church bells were rung despite the overall ban.

I was still visiting Hollymoor as often as I could, and occasionally saw Grandad and Granny, my uncles and aunts but the lives of everyone were changing very much.

Seeing the wounded men at the hospital made me wonder about the aftermath of the war, and I thought of the poor ex-servicemen from the first war who had been gassed or badly wounded, and whose meal cards I had been able to date stamp at Dad's office below the Drill Hall. Thankfully poison gas had not been used although we all still carried gas masks.

The air raids had come to a halt and fire-watching duty once a month was a quiet affair, we played table tennis, made tea and generally kept awake just in case, going home at 7.30 to return for work at nine. For this stint we girls received only four shillings – we never knew how much the men received! The only enemy thank goodness, was an occasional army of cockroaches which appeared under the canteen door. Three girls jumping onto chairs must have been an undignified sight for the male half of the team!

In those bittersweet days there was courtesy and honour, consideration, respect and tolerance, a nation working together, fighting and suffering. I learned a lot about life and death in that terrible period.

I decided at last, in consultation with Mom that I must join one of the services, by choice rather than wait to be conscripted.

John, my brother, was still in Loughborough and Jacqui was to be educated at The Royal Masonic College in Hertfordshire – it meant that Mom would be on her own, like so many women, of course.

My childhood seemed so far away now. I had not seen Fay, Marg or Dorothy, and Peter, my childhood sweetheart was gone but not forgotten. My Godmother, sadly, had passed away a short time after the death of him and my beloved Gip. I now had Dad's bible which would forever remind me of her, and of Dad too, of course.

Things were bad – every spare bit of metal was needed for the war effort. The handsome iron railings round St Philip's Cathedral churchyard had been sawn down and taken away for scrap, along with others from all over the city. Even aluminium pots and pans were called for.

It had been a very bad year but in January 1943 the Germans surrendered in Stalingrad. By May the remnants of Rommel's army had surrendered in North Africa. Politicians began calling for a Second Front but our leader Winston Churchill and his chiefs would know the best time…

One of my friends from the Austin, Marie Flanagan had become a lorry driver in the ATS but after further thoughts I decided to try and join the Women's Land Army. I asked the General Manager, Mr Hill for a morning off and went to the W.L.A offices in Broad Street. There were several selfish reasons why I wanted to become a land girl. One, I had heard that Birmingham girls could get home at weekends and would be posted within the county of Warwickshire, two, I would be able to continue visiting Hollymoor on a Saturday with a bit of luck, and three, I loved the countryside. But would I be able to cope with the hard physical work? I'd filled in a form and obtained three references, one from our family doctor, Dr Renwick, one from Pastor Smith who had run the penny hop at Alton Road church hall in Bournbrook in the air raids, and the third reference from a friend of the family, Uncle Philip, who had known me all my life. I was accepted and obtained my release in August 1943 and was delighted to receive my first posting. I was to report to Squadron Leader Goslett at RAF Wellesbourne Mountford, nr Stratford-upon-Avon. I'd reached another turning point and was about to leave family, friends and familiar surroundings. I felt that at last I would be doing something worthwhile for the war effort, without leaving Mom too far behind.

I'd borrowed Mom's blue, soft-topped case and packed a few clothes, including my two C & A dresses, best black and white crepe dress given to me by Aunt Doll, some black sandals, underwear and two pairs of pyjamas. I also had two pairs of unfashioned rayon stockings – fully-fashioned stockings were a rarity and I wasn't likely (or inclined) to make the acquaintance of any American GIs who it was said could obtain endless supplies of nylons for English girls, at a price no doubt, in some cases.

Mom was on nights the week I was due to leave but she insisted on coming to see me off at Snow Hill Station. I felt guilty but hoped to get back at the weekend, or as soon as possible.

Since Dad's death she had worked long and hard but her serene face never betrayed the tiredness she must have felt. There had been bitterness amongst some of the wounded men from North Africa about various battles fought and lost, and, inevitably about the leadership. But generally they were cheerful, philosophical and optimistic. There continued to be rumours about a Normandy landing but no one had any real idea of when it would take place.

I'd put on my navy edge-to-edge coat over a new white blouse and check shirt which Mom had bought me, and we had gone up to the Bristol Road to wait for a Midland Red bus to take us into Birmingham.

"Are you sure those sandals are comfortable?" Mom looked down at the hinged, wood-soled sandals with the wine-coloured uppers and I said, "They're fine." They were in fact very comfortable, once I'd got used to the idea of wooden soles rather than leather. I would soon have to break in the Land Army shoes and knew my feet would suffer in the process.

In the city we got off the bus and made our way up to Snow Hill Station which fronted onto the Colmore Row. I gave in my railway warrant which had been sent to me and was given a ticket. We found the platform for Stratford-upon-Avon; a dark green engine was already getting up steam on the track. I opened the door of the nearest carriage and once inside opened the window of a compartment.

"I'll try my best to get back at the weekend," I called to Mom above the noise.

Mom said, "Don't worry. Just try and get settled in."

Her eyes were bright with tears and I felt sad as I waved. The train pulled out and I sat down, putting my case on the floor. Four soldiers had come into the compartment and one of them picked up my case and put it on the overhead rack. I nodded my thanks, not at all intimidated by all-male company. I had gone round a great deal with Dad in my early years, meeting his friends, listening to band rehearsals and Club discussions. I got on well with most people and I had never forgotten the poor, broken men in the drill hall kitchens. I'd seen that same look of defeat on the faces of some of the wounded at Hollymoor, men who had fought and lost battles as well as limbs.

The train pulled into the tunnel and presently we were travelling through the ruins of suburban Birmingham where bombing had been heavy. I was looking forward to seeing the countryside but didn't know yet what kind of work I would be doing. I had written 'Market Gardening' as first choice on the form but was ready for anything.

The soldiers began to play cards and I closed my eyes, thinking of the past. Time had flown since I'd left King's Norton Secondary School and it was two years since Dad's death. I'd already had three jobs too. Mom and I had grown very close but I knew she missed John and Jacqueline very much. I'd always recognised and deeply respected her qualities. As a child in Nechells she had been the one to look after the latest addition to the family, organise meals such as they were, in a house with little income. Sometimes there was only two pennyworth of broken biscuits for lunch, she had once told me. I could scarcely imagine such a thing happening in my life. I'd begun to understand why it was that she meticulously ate every scrap of a meal wherever she was. But despite their hardship her family remained united with a strong bond that even death did not break.

1926. *1927.* *1932.*

1940s. *1950s.*

June – A Land Girl Pin-up. June Picken said: "I'm not really local," when Journal feature writer Mel Rolfe asked to see her. She and husband Les, a retired advertising executive, have nevertheless lived at Langar Road, Bingham, for 22 years. For 10 of them, June was secretary at Robert Miles Junior School. This feature, however, dwells more on the war years, when she was June Keppy, in the Land Army.

Parade of a Naval Band in New Street Birmingham. It may have been a victory parade or for 'War Weapons Week'.

Here are two portraits of my late husband Leslie before I met him in 1947. One shows him as an eighteen year old sailor (or able seaman), and the other as a smart petty officer teaching Telegraphy at HMS Ganges in the Midlands.

*The nurses on the ward which Mum worked on during the war. She is the
one on the top right.*

*A garden party held at Hollymoor Hospital, Northfield, Birmingham,
where mum worked as a nurse. The patients were well looked after and
enjoyed concerts and football (if they could play in dressing gowns and in
long grass!). One famous musical star sang for them one night when I had
stayed late. It was Evelyn Laye, dressed in a white dress with a red and
blue sash. There was also an exciting game of Musical Chairs in the
assembly hall with patients slipping all over the place as the music stopped
and the ladies going into hysterics! My mum is the central figure in white,
talking to the man in a dark uniform.*

A cartoon made up by my mum!

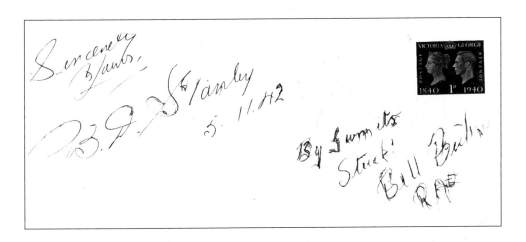

Autographs from two wounded soldiers at Hollymoor Hospital, Northfield,
Birmingham. I visited a ward at weekends as my home war effort!

*My wartime friend, Betty Small, with me in Melton Mowbray Park, 1941.
Pastor Smith had willingly opened up his church hall in Bournbrook to
organise a 'Penny Hop' for the recent input of troops staying at the
temporary high school building a short way away. The dance was at the
Corn Exchange Melton and a super supper was given to thirty girls of
course, and when the Blitz began, on a quietish night, Betty and I would
stand in for the Orchestra, (Firemen), who became very busy each time
there was an air raid.*

*An office friend of mine, Jo Delaney, and I went for a week's break in
Blackpool in 1942. There we met John Mallaber (left) and Gerry, both
engaged in training for Air Crew. A long time after the war I heard, sadly,
that John had been killed when his bomber had been shot down over
Germany. They had been lovely company that sunny afternoon in Blackpool.*

Left: Kath, Jo and myself, on Blackpool Beach, 1945. Kath and I were Land Girls working at RAF Wellesbourne Mountford, near Stratford-upon-Avon. Jo could not get released from her job with the Austin Aero Company. Right: We met Bob, a quiet, shy pilot on the same beach.

Left: Our favourite crew in training. Ken is the pilot on the right. Right: After the war was over I could not settle to an indoor job again after being out of doors for eight months. Lucky for me the caretaker and gardener Mr Cox, with his brother, took me on as a part time jobbing gardener.

May 1915
2 Trenches to Witham Camp 6
6 Camp to Trenches 6
10 Trenches to Bout Reve 3
14 Bout Reve to Trenches 3
18 Trenches to Camp 6
22 Camp to Trenches 6
26 Trenches to Hunting Lodge 3
30 Lodge to Trenches 3
June 1915
3rd Trenches to Romarin 6
7 Romarin to Plœgsteert 6
11 Trenches to Romarin 6
15 Romarin to Trenches 6
19 Trenches to 1875 Farm 2
23 Farm to Trenches 2

Dear Mrs Picken,

Thank you for your letter of 9 February, enclosed is the notebook kept by your late father during his service in the First World War.

It was most interesting to examine your father's notebook, which contains useful details of the locations he visited during his service on the Western Front. He was clearly a well-travelled soldier! I shall be glad to accept the book as a donation to the Museum's archive, where it will now be preserved alongside your own memoir of WLA service.

Top Left: The Fiftieth Anniversary of V.J. V.E. Day and a party was given at the Cheques Inn, Woolsthorpe. We had wartime songs played on the accordion and also some wartime food... Spam for example!
Top Right: A page from my Dad's notebook which he kept during World War I. In 1917 Dad was wounded in action in France and sent home to Southampton Docks on the Hospital Ship S.S. St. David, thence to Birmingham to recuperate. In 1921 he met the lady who would become my mum. They were married in Birmingham in 1922. I was born in 1924. Bottom: A Letter from the Imperial War Museum thanking me for sending them the notebook.

With my daydreaming, time had passed swiftly, and the train was pulling into the station at Stratford-upon-Avon. I stood up and a soldier took down my case, winked and said 'Good luck miss.' I looked at all of them and wished them good luck too. I gave in the ticket at the barrier and went through the waiting room to the street where I could see a girl in a blue battledress standing near a car. She saw me and waved a hand.

"Are you the Land Girl?"

I nodded and she smiled, "Jump in the back, love."

I obeyed. I'd never been chauffeured before!

She told me that her name was Betty and that her home was in Yorkshire. We set off and soon we were passing through a large square where a row of star-studded jeeps stood in front of an attractive timbered hotel.

A flagpole was flying a Stars and Stripes.

"Trust the Yanks to grab the best pub in town," Betty said huffily. Obviously she was not a fan of the USA!

As we moved on I asked, "Betty, am I going to be the only Land Girl at the camp?"

With some relief I learned that two other girls had arrived the previous day.

We crossed a bridge and Betty pointed out a group of swans on the Avon, bright in the September sunshine. I could see the theatre on the far side and I would certainly refresh my memory about Shakespeare if I were to spend time here between buses. Weekends would pass quickly, if I could get home, visiting Hollymoor, hunting for stockings or makeup in shops, helping in the house, looking for some small treat for Mom. Sometimes, surprisingly, there were pomegranates to be had, but never oranges or grapefruit. We did once have a treat when I won a basket of fruit at a dance, and it included a grapefruit.

Whalemeat and snoek appeared in the shops from time to time but were never popular. One pet cat, on approaching her dish containing boiled snoek, jumped backwards in fright, her fur standing on end! And we hated the colour and smell of whale meat.

I'd learned from a reference book in Selly Oak library that Wellesbourne Mountford and Wellesbourne Hastings were adjoining, named after influential families in the Middle Ages. They had improved conditions for agricultural workers but that was all I knew so far.

We passed an estate with a large stone built hall. This, Betty said was Charlecote Hall, where Shakespeare, reputedly poached deer. Betty drove down a quiet main street and pointed out a green corrugated building on the right.

"That's the village hall. There's dancing there most nights. Once a fortnight there's a film show for the local people though we have our own cinema on camp. You'll find plenty to do in your spare time."

"If we have any." I smiled. "I'm expecting to work fairly long hours."

We reached a junction where the road widened and I could see a large white house standing behind a brick wall.

"That's what we call the Waafery," Betty said. "Some of the admin staff sleep here and we pick up our post at the gate lodge."

The main gate to the camp was ahead of us to the right and a sentry approached, saw me in the back of the car and whistled. I tried not to giggle as his friend came to join him. We drove along a road cut out of an expanse of grassland and on the skyline I could see a few planes, standing like neglected toys.

"They're Wellington bombers." Betty explained. "Flying is done at night because the training is for night operations."

I felt a surge of excitement and a twinge of apprehension. We approached a cluster of prefabricated buildings and Betty explained that this was the heart of the camp where the powers that be had their offices. In the forecourt there were flowerbeds, and roses climbed a white trellis. To the right was a guardroom with bars on some of the windows. A Royal Air Force flag was flying on top of a white flagpole not far away.

Notices on doors indicated Stores, the Fire Department and Maintenance Department offices. We got out of the car and I followed Betty into the main building where she knocked at a door marked 'Administrative Officer. Squadron Leader C. Goslett.' My heart thumped madly.

A brisk voice called 'Come in' and I found myself standing in front of a large desk behind which stood a tall, immaculately uniformed figure. I saw keen blue eyes and grey hair.

Betty saluted, "Miss Keppy, sir," and withdrew.

'Oh Lord!' I thought. I suddenly remembered my first day at school when I'd been called out to the front of the class and given two strokes of the cane… Oh heck… was I on trial? I gripped the handles of my case and handbag just that little bit tighter…

"You're very young!"

As the Squadron Leader spoke my heart sank into my wooden-soled sandals. This wasn't a good start! I smiled, immediately resolving to put up my hair and add a few years to my appearance. The Squadron Leader's words had seemed more an accusation than a greeting.

"I am nineteen, sir," I ventured, with all the wisdom of a dowager, I hoped.

He asked about my family and what I'd been doing since the outbreak of war. He did have to be careful about who he employed, I realised that but my references had been well received at the recruiting office.

Then he said, "I'll take you to meet your colleagues, Miss Keppy." I picked up my case and followed him out of the office into the corridor, to a rear door and along a narrow path until we reached a large hangar. Opposite was a patch of ground where four people were digging up something. It looked like… leeks! I'd never seen leeks actually growing!

A pick up truck stood nearby and a stocky figure in blue battledress, with three stripes came to us, saluting smartly.

"Sergeant Lenner – meet Miss Keppy, the third of your three ladies." The Sergeant looked me over with dark brown eyes and I thought 'I bet he could be mean and moody.'

"Mornin'" he drawled in what I took to be a West Country or Gloucestershire accent. He beckoned to the others and they came over. The Squadron Leader introduced me. "Miss O'Neil and Miss Baker, meet Miss Keppy."

The first girl was fair and slim, with blue eyes, the second girl dark and plump, with curly hair and brown eyes. They smiled; we all shook hands and I knew we would be friends. I didn't catch the names of the two ACs but they seemed quite pleasant.

"Sergeant, find Miss Keppy a cycle will you? I'm putting in a requisition for WAAF issue today." The Squadron Leader stood smiling at the three of us and took his leave, the men saluting.

After shaking down a couple of sacks of leeks the sergeant said, as if I wasn't there, "You'd better take 'er up the 'ut. She can get changed before dinner." The girls scraped the mud from their Wellington boots and grinned at me, then collected their cycles from near the hangar. The ACs put the sacks onto the truck with the tools and drove away, the sergeant with them.

Miss O'Neil smiled, "What's your first name?"

"June," I said.

"I'm Kath." Then the dark girl said, "I'm Muriel."

We walked together through the camp and I learned that both Kath and Muriel had been in the Women's Land Army for three years. Kath was a Birmingham girl, Muriel from Coventry. I was the rookie, also the youngest. Kath was twenty-six and Muriel twenty-four.

"I'm looking forward to working out of doors," I ventured. Kath looked at me with a wry smile. "The weather's good at the moment but it can be hard going," Muriel added, "You'll find you've got muscles you never knew existed!"

"It's not so bad," Kath interposed quickly. "We don't want to put you off, June."

As we walked I learned that Muriel had been doing dairy work at Long Marston, a village not far away.

"Is it true that cows lean on you when you milk them?" I asked remembering Mr Biggs, one of the fire watching team at the Austin gleefully warned me of this phenomenon when he learned of my intention to join the service.

"Quite true," Muriel laughed, "and they're no lightweights either!"

Kath had done general work at Southam but had not been too happy. She had put in for a posting. Muriel had become engaged to a soldier stationed in Long Marston but he had been sent overseas. She had felt lonely so she too had applied for another job.

"Have you got a boyfriend?" Muriel asked. I shook my head.

"I write to a few ex-patients from the hospital where Mom works, that's all. And an RAF friend who is a POW in Germany."

We were passing several rows of wooden huts which were raised from the ground, with steps leading up to each door. There were curtains at the windows and I was curious to hear about them.

"Air Crews," Kath said, "Their bat women have the hut next to ours."

"I thought it was all bat men" I said, surprised. Muriel laughed, "They're a tough crowd of girls from what we've seen so far."

We were now on a narrow path and to our right was a spinney with tall trees. I could hear wood pigeons cooing. The sky was quiet and Kath confirmed that flying was done at night. We reached a lane and I was surprised to see that there was no guard.

"All that fuss at the main gate," Kath laughed, "yet there's a dozen ways of getting into camp. Isn't it daft?"

We crossed the lane and walked towards a row of black huts which were placed end to end. The overhanging branches of mature trees made it seem dark but there was a glimpse of a golden cornfield at the back.

Kath and Muriel parked their cycles outside the door of the last but one hut and I waited while Kath opened it.

"This used to be the WAAF Sergeants' hut," she explained, "They've gone down the lane to a cottage so we've been put in here. We're lucky though. We do have a room each."

I found myself in a central corridor, with three half-glazed doors on each side. The girls had chosen rooms overlooking the cornfield so I did the same."

"There's one thing we don't like, though," Muriel said, "we've got to leave all our doors unlocked when we go out in the morning, for the Orderly Officer of the day to inspect the hut."

She opened the door of my room. "We have to fold our bedding RAF style before we go out."

She indicated a pile of sheets and blankets on the bed near the door, and my heart dropped a little as I looked round the room. An ugly looking black stove stood in one corner, its flue pipe rising through the ceiling. The bare walls were painted pale green and apart from the metal-framed bed the only furniture was a wooden chair. For the purpose of hanging clothes a single nail had been driven into the wall about five feet from the floor. On the bed were three square objects which Kath said were known as 'biscuits', in other words the mattress. There were two kit bags, one large one which stood near the bed, and a small version on the bed. Muriel loosened the top of the large one.

"This is your kit, June," she said. Then she picked up the small object. "This is a palliasse if you haven't seen one before. You're supposed to lie your weary head on it at night but we're going to bring a pillow from home. I should do the same if I were you."

I felt the palliasse critically, "I see what you mean."

Kath pulled back the black curtains and we could see a man on a red tractor working in the field. The sky was blue and my heart lifted. I was in the countryside at last.

I smiled at the two girls, "I just hope I can fold those things properly. I've always been hopeless with straight lines and edges."

"It's the only regulation which applies to us, apart from the ritual at the main gate," Kath said. "What do you think of the Squadron Leader?"

"I like him," I nodded, "but he said I look very young. Is that bad?" Muriel laughed, "No! How old are you, June?"

"I was nineteen in July," I answered.

I looked at my new companions and felt very lucky that my first posting had brought me to work with such nice girls. Kath had seemed the more serious of the two, but I suspected that Muriel hid deep emotions under bubbly exterior.

"Unpack your kit," Kath said, "and come down to the Ritz when you're ready."

"The Ritz? What's that?" I asked, laughing.

She pointed through the window and I could see the roof of a small building.

"The ablutions! The water's cold and the chains don't pull, otherwise it's just like the Ritz!"

They advised me what to put on, and went to their own rooms for their soap and towels. I opened the top of the large bag and pulled the items out one by one. First came the 'pork pie' hat in a shade of fawn, and I tried it on with some trepidation. How could I anchor it to my mass of unruly hair? Next came the overcoat in similar colour. It didn't look too bad. I'd seen girls in Birmingham wearing them and they seemed rather short in length. It was good quality material. Next came the item I'd been longing to wear – the deep green, V necked woollen jumper with long sleeves. Two pairs of dungarees came next, two cow gowns, two pairs of breeches, one in cord and one in twill, two pairs of long fawn socks, a cream poplin shirt with long sleeves, two short-sleeved Aertex shirts, a pair of brown walking out shoes and what the… a pair of black army type boots with studded soles! On my size sixes they definitely would not look elegant!

I thought of my childhood – the built-up 'sensible' shoes I always had to wear. How I'd longed for some shiny black ankle-strap shoes!

Since leaving school I'd had a few pairs of better shoes, with Cuban heels, or wedges, but my feet inevitably suffered with the breaking-in process.

I sighed and resigned myself to putting on the Wellington boots standing near the bed. The brown shoes would have to be broken in sooner or later, when the weather became too cold for sandals.

I took off my coat, blouse, skirt and underslip, stockings and roll-on, and put on a pair of the dungarees, an Aertex shirt and some socks, with the boots. Opening the blue case I sorted out my towel and the bar of Imperial Leather soap I'd managed to buy in Littlewoods in New Street. I made my way out of the hut, starting down the path. Suddenly I heard a lorry passing, men's voices singing 'O Sole Mio.' I didn't dare look round, I just ran down the path!

Kath came out laughing. "I meant to warn you, June. The Italian POWs pass through here twice a day. They're always singing; apparently!"

"They did sound lovely," I admitted.

Presently when we were all ready we left the hut and walked past the spinney into camp. Becoming a cyclist would certainly be a case of trial and error! We arrived at the Airmen's Mess hall, a large building with tables seating eight, the men at one end, the WAAFS at the other. Kath smiled, "We had our initiation yesterday, now it's your turn." As we shuffled along the counter with our trays there were whistles from the men and cold stares from the WAAFS. I'd been given my 'irons' (knife, fork and spoon) and a thick white cup. Muriel and Kath had taken theirs from what looked like pump bags and I remembered I still had mine from King's Norton School.

My first RAF meal consisted of braised beef, piles of potatoes, cabbage, carrots and gravy, and served at the same time a dish of rice pudding. Tea was collected from a central urn where there were sinks for washing plates and irons, and a row of bins for uneaten food. The food looked good but none of us were sure about the tea – it could have been cocoa, judging by its colour! We took our trays to a table near a window but no WAAFS joined us.

Muriel whispered, "I don't think we're going to be very popular. Nobody came to join us yesterday either."

We were shocked to see the amount of food which was wasted, and it was heartbreaking to think of the size of the civilian rations. But generally people seemed to be healthy and I was sure it was the British spirit that kept us going.

After lunch we went back to the field near HQ where there were still leeks to dig up. The sergeant had, on the Squadron Leader's instructions, found me a cycle. He grinned wickedly as I gazed in awe at the machine.

"This'll do yer till the other comes. It ain't so bad is it?"

It was a very old, sit-up-and-beg model for men, with a high saddle and only one complete foot pedal. I thought I'd better own up.

"To tell you the truth, sergeant, I've never ridden a bike in my life."

He thought this a huge joke and roared with laughter.

"Well, there's nothing like learnin' the 'ard way is there?"

I glanced at the other two men and felt that they had some sympathy. Kath and Muriel were not too happy but promised, "We'll help on and off."

The sergeant went off to deal with some mysterious business and the two men began digging. Kath, Muriel and I stood looking at the bicycle.

"He could have found something better than this." Muriel tried the brake lever. "There must be some spare WAAF ones knocking about the camp."

Kath scowled, "I suspect that he's got a strange sense of humour."

We joined the men and dug up the remaining leeks for transport to the Stores. By five-thirty I was aching all over, blisters were forming on my hands and my feet ached. But we enjoyed our meal of sausage and chips in the mess. We walked back to the hut pushing our bikes. I found the sit-up-and-beg very difficult to handle. There had been no chance of a bath that first night but we had been told we could use the WAAF officers' bathrooms. I was tired and decided to go to bed early. Kath and Muriel were used to the work out of doors but they too felt ready for an early night. We talked for a while and I learned about their families. Muriel told us about her fiancé Ian who came from Invergordon in the north of Scotland. He had been stationed at Long Marston; they had fallen in love and become engaged. She had dreaded the day when he would be sent overseas and when it came she was very lonely. So she had decided to put in for another job.

I told them about Dad dying so suddenly two years earlier and about Mom working at Hollymoor since 1939. I said, "I'm hoping we can get home at weekends but the Squadron Leader took all the week's coupons."

Kath nodded, "I know. I suppose it would be difficult for him. There may be times when we may want to stay on the camp."

"I never thought of that," I replied. "Do you think we will get home at all?"

Kath nodded, "No chance Friday nights. We'll have to catch the first available bus from here on a Saturday morning but with a bit of luck we should be in Brum by two."

Muriel told us that she would have to go to Leamington Spa for her connection to Coventry.

We parted company at ten and I undressed, putting on my pyjamas. I lay for a while looking through the open curtains at the sky. I'd had a happy life apart from losing Peter, Dad, Aunt Jess, Godmother and Gip, and my school friend Jean who had been killed driving an ambulance. Time had flown since leaving King's Norton Secondary School and I prayed the worst of the war was over. Although I had not attended church on a regular basis I had strong faith and at the back of my mind there was the childhood search. The naïve dreams of childhood had passed and for the time being I'd accepted that paintings of Jesus were all I would have.

I slept well that first night even though it was in a strange, rather hard bed. In the morning at 6.30 I was awakened by an unfamiliar sound – Reveille coming loud and clear over the Tannoy system. We washed at the Ritz and dressed for the day's work. We were to work at the Waafery that first morning, for me at least. Breakfast would be the only meal we would ever have at the Waafery if we were working there. The kitchen closed at 9.30 and all other meals were eaten by everyone at the mess.

Well, there had to be a first time for everything! Kath and Muriel helped me onto the high placed saddle of the bike and gave me a gentle push, to set me off down the lane. "We'll keep our fingers crossed!" they called as the bike gathered speed. 'Oh heck!' I thought, 'I hope I don't meet any traffic!'

Near the bottom of the lane I squeezed the brake lever – nothing happened. There was only one thing to do if I didn't want to be flattened against the Waafery wall. I threw myself off onto a grass verge to my left. Rather shaken, I picked myself up and waited for Kath and Muriel who arrived at a more leisurely pace. This hair-raising ritual would have to be gone through every time we worked at the Waafery. Working on camp would be much easier – I could mount the bike by the spinney fence and cycle along the level path into the camp at a controlled speed, hopefully!

We had a few days working in the greenhouses then we received a message to meet the men one morning after breakfast outside the Mess. The air was fresh and clear, the sun bright and gold and as we walked past the spinney we could hear bird songs unfamiliar to our city-trained ears. After breakfast we joined Jack and Oliver who were waiting with the pick-up truck and the necessary tools. We climbed into the back and Jack sat with us, Oliver did the driving.

"Where are we going, Jack," Muriel asked as the truck sped along the perimeter.

He shouted, "Beet field beyond the sprout field!"

I put my hands over my ears and pulled a face, "It's a bit parky."

"Wait till winter, me flowers. It's like being at the North Pole out here!"

"Thanks a lot," Kath groaned. The truck passed several Wellington bombers which were being serviced and the mechanics waved to us. They all seemed so cheerful and hard working. I was surprised at the length of the runways but bombers needed a lot of room for take off, I realised that. Jack pointed out several potato fields then another showing lighter green.

"Sprouts! Just the job for the cold weather," he smiled.

"All those potatoes," Kath pointed out, "that spells hard work."

Potato lifting would be new to Muriel as well as to me.

At last the truck stopped at a green verge and we got off the truck with our bikes, tools and buckets. As far as we could see there were weeds and thistles, almost waist-high.

"Where are the beetroot Jack?" Kath asked.

"I'll give you three guesses!" he grinned at her. Muriel stared at him, "You don't mean we've got to dig up all those weeds and thistles to get at them?"

He took a fork, "It's not so bad." He dug up a few thistles, spearing a woody looking beetroot at the same time.

"You're cheating!" Kath said, "the ground's soft at the edge. What's it like in the middle eh?"

Oliver handed her the fork, his round face wreathed in smiles.

"Do your best, girls." He climbed into the cab and Jack joined him.

"Aren't you staying to help us?" Muriel said indignantly.

"Things to do, me flowers," Jack grinned as Oliver started the engine.

"And what about our tea?" Kath asked. We couldn't survive without our tea!

Jack handed out a large oblong tin. "Fetch it in this."

I took it from him. "Where from?"

"The mess of course. You'll have to toss for it as to who goes. It's a long ride back on a bike!"

The truck moved off and the men waved,

"Thanks for nothing!" Kath shouted but her words were lost on the wind.

We sat down on the grass. "Trust the sergeant to find us a horrible job." Muriel groaned. "I wonder what he's doing this morning?"

Two hours of hard digging produced nothing more worthwhile than a few wrinkled beetroot, a pile of magnificent thistles and three pairs of blistered hands.

At last we flopped down onto the grass. "Who's going for tea?" Kath said wearily.

Against my better judgement I said, "I'll go."

Kath was anxious about the bike's safety. "Please. June, be careful."

I laughed uneasily. "I must get all the practice I can."

Muriel warned, "Keep to the perimeter and watch out for planes."

It would be a good ten minutes ride each way, I calculated, as I set off with the Tate and Lyle treacle tin wedged between the handlebars. We were becoming used to aircraft noise and it was not until I passed the mechanics that I realised they were laughing at something behind me. I glanced over my shoulder and nearly fell off the bike in fright! Taxiing about twenty yards behind me was a Fairey Battle plane and I could see the pilot's grinning face!

I pedalled faster but he stayed close behind, and reaching the end of the perimeter I got off the bike, turned and shook my fist at him. He winked and expertly turned the plane round, taxiing away. This was my first encounter with Whitey, the camp daredevil, an instructor who had completed one tour of operations. Charming and mischievous, Whitey was loved by all who worked with him, and we were to see quite a lot of him at the pub and the village hall. Since, to give him his due, he did eventually apologise to me for scaring me that day!

Being chased by a daredevil in a plane had taxed my old bike to its limit, and I was very relieved when the Squadron Leader called me to his office soon afterwards to present me with my WAAF issue ladies bike.

He enquired, "How are you getting along, Miss Keppy?"

I said, "Fine thank-you, sir."

"Are you sure it's not too much for you?" he pursued the matter. I assured him all was well and he said that I must bear any expenses for the bike myself and return it in good order if I left, which was fair enough.

The Waafery had obviously once been a charming private home, and, like the Middlemoor Emigration Home where I'd worked for the Austin, had been requisitioned for the war. There was a prefabricated cookhouse at the back, and a single-storey NAAFI. A winding path led to an apple orchard, and we were to find unexpected beauty amongst the old trees, violets and snowdrops in their seasons.

There were greenhouses where tomatoes and cucumbers were being grown, and a boiler house which we nicknamed 'The Black Hole.' This provided heating for the greenhouses. Behind a wooden door set in high brick wall was a kitchen garden, where there were rows of radishes, onions, beetroot, and mysterious crop which we learned where Jerusalem artichokes. We went one morning into the enclosed garden with hoes and forks, and Oliver instructed us to dig up the radishes. But it was too late – they had gone woody.

"What a waste," I observed. Mom had often grown a few rows of radishes at our house in Wardwards Lane and had let me pull them up when they were ready. Such pleasure found in small things!

From time to time we cast our eyes towards a hothouse which backed onto the wall of the house. Bunches of black grapes hung in profusion, an exotic sight for Warwickshire!

"Any chance of a bunch, Oliver?" Kath asked hopefully.

He shook his head, smiling, "They all go to Sick Quarters for patients."

"Oh yes?" said Kath unbelieving.

At mid-morning Sarge arrived and took us into the largest of the greenhouses. Most of the tomatoes were ready for picking. The smell of the greenhouse was familiar to me as Mom had grown tomatoes and cucumbers in the small lean-to greenhouse at the back of our house in Weoley Hill.

"Put 'em in boxes," instructed Sarge, "I'll fetch 'em later on." He went away and the morning passed pleasantly. Oliver put a few on one side for us to take to the hut. Kath said, "Oh great! We can do toast with them at night for our supper. Have you got a spare mess tin to cook them in?"

"I'll see what I can do," he promised.

It took us the best part of a day to dig up all the remaining leeks and we asked Oliver what was going to happen about the beet field.

"Sarge will plough it over. It's too far gone, you'll be glad to know."

We planted cabbages in the plot of ground at the back of the Officers' Mess, after digging the ground where the leeks had been growing.

Sarge had been teaching me how to dig and I quite enjoyed it once I knew how. My body was becoming accustomed to the work and my hands were hardening.

The three of us had been well accepted by the permanent members of staff but were still something of a novelty to the contingents of Canadian flyers who came for their night flight training.

Kath and Muriel had, like me, led quite busy lives and had experienced air raids on their weekend leaves in Birmingham and Coventry.

My left foot, injured during Birmingham's longest air raid had begun to suffer with the wearing of Wellington boots and it had been a relief to change into sandals in the evening. I knew that as the weather grew colder I would have to wear the brown shoes and was not looking forward to it. One day, after work, I was in my room resting the foot and Muriel came in. She looked at it, very concerned, "I think you should see the MO. It's very swollen, June."

"I dread having to ask Sarge," I frowned.

"Never mind him! It does need attention," Kath had come into the room and agreed with Muriel.

The following morning I plucked up the courage and said, "Sarge, could I see the MO please? My left foot's giving me trouble."

He grumbled and growled but said he would arrange an appointment for me with the Medical Officer.

There was not a wide variety of food served in the mess but what there was was good. There was curry or stew at lunchtime, always with lots of potatoes, sometimes rice. When ever we walked into the mess the men would start chanting, "No meat and all potatoes!"

The evening meal was more adventurous. There were plenty of chips, tasty sausages, Spam, baked beans or fried onions. The dried egg looked more like piccalilli than scrambled egg, and fresh eggs were non-existent during the week. However there was a shell egg for everyone for Sunday breakfast. We missed this treat because we went home, but going home was worth more than an egg to us!

Aircrews were given bacon, kidneys, eggs and chips after flying and if we happened to be near the Officers' Mess kitchens we enjoyed the almost forgotten smells.

The WAAFS were still unfriendly, especially the counter-hands in the mess hall. One day as we filed along with our trays and were being met with the usual indifference Kath said, in a burst of temper which surprised us all, "We'd have you know that we don't get our food for free here! We have to pay one third of our hard earned wage to the Royal Air Force for our board and lodging so we're not left with much, I can assure you!"

There was a hush as the outburst sunk in. After that we were treated a great deal better, in fact were offered second and third helpings as if our very lives depended on it... well ... they did! We were always hungry and looked forward to snacks whenever and wherever we could get them. We enjoyed eating at the village hall and some lunchtimes would have a quick drink at the Stag, sitting outside at a small table overlooking the street.

The mornings were still bright, clear and quite mild and as yet we felt no hardship in getting up at six thirty to the sound of Reveille, washing in near cold water at the Ritz and cycling to breakfast at the mess or the Waafery. The cornfield was still golden, although the harvest had been gathered in. Only a few bales of straw remained, standing like sentinels on the wide, undulating field. It had been many years since I'd seen such a sight, then only from the top of the Lickey Hills as a schoolgirl.

Working out of doors was giving me a sense of freedom hitherto unknown in an office. I knew I'd made the right choice... but the war was still a long way from ending...

We worked hard, as all land girls did, but unlike the majority we had compensation in the form of excellent camp entertainment and the village activities as well. We loved working at the Waafery. There seemed to be something mysterious and exciting about the old orchard and the kitchen garden behind the high brick wall, even though the crops had been sadly neglected.

Sarge had arranged for me to see Flight Lieutenant Russell, the MO and I felt nervous as I found myself face-to-face with a very good looking fair-haired man in uniform who sat at a large desk picking at a bunch of black grapes...

"Good morning, miss. Have a grape!"

"Oh thank-you sir," I accepted with alacrity and he said, "Now, let's see this foot of yours."

Feeling embarrassed I took off my boot and sock and he examined the foot with interest. I felt myself blushing. My 'plates of meat' had never been an elegant part of my anatomy!

"How did this happen, missie?" he asked softly.

I told him how I had been at a dance, at the Lodge Hill Road Sports Pavilion in Selly Oak. When an air raid began we were told to go across the sports field to the public shelter. Unfortunately there had been a large hole in the ground which no one had mentioned and I was the first to fall into it, followed by several soldiers who had been attending the dance in their army boots. One stepped on my left foot and it had swelled like a balloon. A sergeant had used a sling from his first aid kit, dipped in a muddy puddle and applied it to my foot, then he and two soldiers had helped me up the Bristol Road and flagged down a lorry. They asked the driver to take us all to our house. Luckily the soldiers knew Mom and Dad and they said they would go along to the shelter in Shenley Fields Road and wait there for them. Mom and Dad had been visiting Jacqui in Wythall but had been unable to get back because of a fallen land mine.

We were thrilled to receive other invitations to dances and parties which were coming up in the near future, so hard work was always compensated by the thought of good times to come. We considered ourselves very lucky to have so much to do in our spare time. Other Land Girls in the area had nothing but supper and bed to look forward to after a hard day's work.

We sat one evening in the village hall refreshment room munching as usual. I was always hungry and in those halcyon days never gained weight. Kath was very slim but quite strong, Muriel, small and plump, was very fit and active. I was gradually growing accustomed to the outdoor life though I'd never been sporty or full of boundless energy.

Muriel sipped her tea and said wistfully, "Oh I do wish Ian was back home." She wrote to him every day and he wrote back as often as could, censors permitting. "I'm so glad I'm here with you both."

"We're glad too," Kath said. I felt suddenly ashamed at the way we had teased her, doing silly things like hiding his photograph, or putting it upside down in its frame. I suddenly realised that if I was in love with a man who was away on active service I wouldn't feel like putting up with silly pranks. I said, and meant it wholeheartedly, "Muriel, we pray every night for his safe return. You must believe that."

"Bless you," she said, her brown eyes filling with tears. I think we all felt very close to one another at that moment.

A day or two later I went for my first treatment at Sick Quarters and was greeted by a fair-haired nurse whose name was Jill. She gave me a cup of tea and chatted, and just then a Flight Sergeant came in.

"Hey aren't I the lucky lad! Good morning miss. Call me Flight."

I said good morning rather self-consciously and he asked me to take off my boot and sock. "It's quite swollen," he remarked. "The MO says you are to have some treatment for a week or so. It might help."

I knew that Sarge would not be very pleased but hard luck – I would be enjoying a break from routine and the girls wouldn't mind. I got to know Jill quite well. Her fiancé had been reported missing over Germany and she was putting in for posting from Wellesbourne Mountford camp. I couldn't see that moving to another camp would help her state of mind.

One evening as we went to mess for our meal Sarge caught us up.

"You girls – get down to the Waafery first thing after yer breakfast! I want yer to rake out that mound of coke that's there."

"Mound of coke? Where?" Kath asked.

He was impatient. "You'll see if yer look hard enough. It's in the orchard of course! Where else would it be?" We looked at one another and said nothing. He continued, "Olly'll be there with the tools. Rake it all out and get it to the boiler house. The coal ain't come and it'll keep things moving for a day or two."

He was off before we could say 'boo.' The following morning we cycled down to the Waafery for breakfast. There was bacon for breakfast! Excitedly we collected our bread, marge, marmalade and sugar as usual and Janet gave us each a generous helping of bacon and fried bread. What a treat it was! Then we had our usual 'seconds' of bread, marge and sugar but not bacon. That would have been too greedy of us to expect!

Presently we went round to the potting shed where Oliver was waiting with three rakes and six buckets.

Kath said, "We've never seen a mound of coke, Olly."

We parked our bikes and following him round into the orchard. "Will it be worth the effort?" Muriel wanted to know too.

He grinned, "Sarge thinks so. Do your best girls."

He showed us a grassy bank which we'd never noticed before. After an hour's raking we had unearthed a motley assortment of objects including bottles and jars, a forage cup, a rusty mess tin and a pair of braces. Nothing of any use to us but the boiler would be richer by a couple of dozen buckets of coke as Sarge had predicted!

Some time later, Squadron Leader Goslett decided that there was not enough greenery around the centre of camp and he ordered two dozen cypress trees. Olly and Jack began planting, some alongside the Airmen's Mess and they certainly improved the look of the area. On the third day as we helped with the work, Sarge arrived, grinning all over his face. "Now then you girls. Like some toast this morning would yer?"

We all looked at one another. Toast! It was probably a regular event in his life. He knew his way round, did Sarge!

Full of self-importance he led the way into the Airmen's Mess boiler house and we looked round in amazement. This was very different from the 'Black Hole' at the Waafery! This was a large room, resplendent with gleaming tiles and brass. A huge modern furnace was at one side and we could see a brass toasting fork hanging on the wall nearby. Sarge took it down and handed it to Muriel, then he opened the furnace door, the heat almost knocked us back.

"I'll get yer bread," he announced and went through an inner door. Presently he came back with a pile of thickly sliced bread and handed it to me.

"Where's the marge?" I asked. He grinned, "Ask Jock in the kitchen. He'll see you all right."

He left, and Muriel began to toast the slices as I handed them to her. Then when the pile was done we all went through into the kitchen for the margarine. Obviously it was elevenses for the staff there too. A small man in a white coat came over to us grinning toothlessly at Muriel. Obviously he had an eye for her charms!

"D'ye want some butter, hen?"

This was obviously Jock, and we all giggled.

"Yes please," Muriel said, attaching no importance to the word 'butter' – all we ever saw was margarine!

Jock unlocked a tall cupboard and took out some oblong packets. He put them on a table and unwrapped them, then took a knife and cut slices as thick as the bread itself. It was… real butter! Sheer luxury! Utter extravagance! But who were we to argue? We made the most of it, savouring every mouthful. Never again would we turn our noses up at plain bread and butter when the war was over!

Inevitably the days grew colder and we welcomed work in the greenhouses, drinking our morning tea in the 'Black Hole' and warming our feet on the hot pipes. This, of course, was a big mistake, and we all developed chilblains. But country folk had a remedy for most things and Olly's advise to us was to rub the offending chilblains with raw onion – painful but effective!

After the tomatoes had finished ripening we prepared trays for growing mustard and cress. This grew quickly, and was just quickly consumed in the Sergeants' and Officers' messes. However, the lettuce we planted never grew to maturity – the seedlings we pricked out every day were always eaten the same night by creeping little night visitors!

Two WAAFS who were friendly with us were 'Taffy One' and 'Taffy Two,' both Batwomen and twins. One day, 'Taffy One' called us over to the open window of a room she was cleaning and we looked with interest. The walls were covered with pictures of glamour girls in bathing suits.

"Whose room is this?" we enquired.

"Whitey's" Taffy One replied. "See that photo in the silver frame by the bed? That's his wife and he adores her! But it doesn't stop him having all these pin ups. Men!"

Whitey, bless him, was to disgrace himself again. One day Squadron Leader Goslett was entertaining a visiting Air Marshal and showing him round the camp. Suddenly the Fairey Battle appeared doing a loop the loop very dangerously low. Gossy was furious and grounded Whitey as punishment for three weeks. He drowned his sorrows at the King's Head then wandered alcoholically and innocently into the ladies cloakroom at the village hall! But Whitey was too valuable a pilot to waste and was allowed to fly again after three days. Later he produced nylon stockings for all the ladies in the refreshment room who had earlier frowned on his misdeeds. One smile and twitch of his huge blond moustache and they all went weak at the knees!

Although we tried very hard we could not soften the WAAFS attitude towards us. Perhaps it was because we were treated almost like VIP's, invited to functions, given special chaperons, and of course were free to wear our dresses in the evenings. Everyone could use the NAAFI, but WAAFS could not go into the Sergeants' Mess unless they were sergeants themselves, and were never allowed into the Officers' Mess unless they actually worked there, or were officers.

A week later MO Flight Lieutenant Russell escorted us all to see another film. He was a charming man and very popular, so there was a respectful silence as we all walked in together. I still felt very embarrassed about him seeing my not very elegant foot!

On Sunday afternoons Kath and I met outside St Martin's Church in the Bull Ring to catch the 2 o'clock Red bus to Stratford-upon-Avon. We had about an hour to wait for our Wellesbourne connection so we walked round the pretty town or went to a café, Morris's, in the square, for tea and cakes. After

"Are you shooting a line?" I demanded.

"No," he laughed. "I work for Walter Bird in civvy street. He's a society photographer. I'm always on the look out for suitable subjects. Will you sit for me?"

I was flattered but cautious, "I will if my friends can have some as well. We're always being asked for photos round the camp."

"Certainly," he said eagerly. He fixed a tentative date three weeks away or after he'd finished the current course. We were just about to leave when we heard a commotion at the bar next door.

"What's happened?" Kath asked. Bob shook his head. "Just a few civvies, always in there causing trouble, accusing instructors of sitting out the war."

"How awful!" We were indignant. "I'd call them fifth columnists," Muriel said.

He told us about the instructors who had already completed a tour of ops. Their rest period was used to teach other flyers about night flying on operations.

At closing time Bob and Don walked up the lane with us, their own quarters were beyond the spinney. Don reminded us about the photo date and in the hut we talked excitedly about clothes before retiring to bed.

The following morning Stan the Sergeant in charge of the Fire Department came to see us at the Waafery.

"Sarge says one of you is to come with us to the hut. Who is it to be then?"

"June," the others said. I couldn't refuse so I climbed onto the gleaming fire tender on which sat three men and Stan drove. I couldn't help giggling. All this fuss just to clean out three chimneys!

Stan drove the tender up the lane and stopped opposite our hut. Then he instructed on of the men to climb onto the roof with his equipment. This consisted of a large stone tied onto a long piece of string! The man lowered this up and down each of the three chimneys whilst the other men stood with me in each room supervising the fall out of soot. Later we all went back to the Waafery where Kath and Muriel were cutting mustard and cress in the large greenhouse. Then the three of us cycled up to the admin. area where we helped Olly and Jack tie up the climbing roses. We pretended to ignore signals coming from behind the barred windows of the guardroom where a few wrongdoers were languishing for various terms of imprisonment. They all looked such innocent lambs!

The Squadron Leader had another bright idea shortly after this. He decided that his admin. staff were not getting enough exercise, sitting at their desks all day. He decided that it was bad for them so he ordered Bob the P.T. instructor to take them through physical jerks each morning before breakfast. We thought it was very funny until Bob suggested that we join in!

"You're joking," Kath said indignantly. "We get enough exercise thank-you very much Bob!"

Reluctantly he agreed then went to break the news to the unsuspecting admin. staff. I was somewhat relieved as my own P.E. sessions at school had been disastrous!

Our welfare was always of great concern to the boys on camp. Many of them expressed concern about us having to sleep in an isolated hut but it didn't occur to them that their female counterparts were doing just that. The WAAFS worked long and hard, many of them coping with large motor vehicles. I often wondered how Marie, my petite fire watching friend had coped in the A.T.S. as a truck driver.

When next I went to Sick Quarters Jill told me that she was about to be posted but still had heard nothing of her missing fiancé. I wished her well and prayed that he would come back safely. She was such a lovely person.

One morning we were working on a patch of ground near the Officers' Mess when the Squadron Leader came along with Sarge. They went to look at an enclosure at the end of the land and after 'Gossy' had gone Sarge came to us, grinning.

"You girls are going to have some little friends."

"Little friends?" We were delighted. Livestock would make a nice change from crops.

"What are we having then, Sarge?" Kath asked.

"Tell us please!" added Muriel.

"Wait and see," was his reply. After he'd gone we discussed possibilities. Cows? Sheep? Pigs? No!

We decided it might be chickens but time would tell. Our chilblains were well on the way to being cured by Olly's remedy and it was quite a relief. We had learned never to put our feet on hot pipes again!

We now needed to wear more clothes, not only for work but also in bed. We woke some nights feeling very cold indeed. Unless the fuel situation improved we would have to consider moving to the village. We had begun to hear strange noises and these, in addition to the hooting of owls and the squeaking of bats did nothing to dispel our unease. We sat one night and talked about moving from the hut. Would the Squadron Leader allow it? Would anyone take us in and what would it cost us? These were the main questions, but we decided to wait a while longer, at least until the cold became unbearable. We knew most of the RAF personnel who lived beyond the spinney but there was also a Belgian army camp, and the Italian prisoners of war's quarters. Although we enjoyed their beautiful Neapolitan songs as the truck passed our hut each day we were becoming very embarrassed by the growing intensity of the stares we were receiving!

At last Sarge broke the news that the 'little friends' were going to be goslings, twenty-four of them! This was another brain-child of the Squadron Leader, and inevitably the catchphrase 'Gossy and his Goslings' went round the camp like wild fire. None of us had any idea how to look after geese and Olly warned, "You'll have to watch your fingers. Very vicious geese can be!"

Nevertheless it was something new and exciting to look forward to. A few days later Sarge said, "Get yourselves to that patch behind the Officers' Mess and cut them marrers! Olly'll show you where them geese are a-goin".

We had already guessed where the geese were going because we had seen him with the Squadron Leader looking at the enclosure. As ordered we went along to cut the marrows in which our names looked very impressive, having grown large with the vegetables!

The Airmen's Mess staff lost their resentment to us at last and were now quite friendly, indulging us with toast and butter whenever we happened to be working near the Airmen's Mess. The Sergeants' Mess cooks too, always produced snacks, the giant sausage rolls and mugs of hot cocoa. However, the Officers' Mess kitchen staff were a different kettle of fish. We had spent a lot of time working close to the mess but had never been offered even a glass of water! The Officers' Mess kitchen staff went about their work with their noses in the air whilst our noses, if within sniffing distance, pressed longingly against a windowpane, drawn by the almost-forgotten smell of kidneys, bacon and eggs, which were always given to the flyers. On this particular day, however, whilst we gathered the marrows we discussed ways of infiltrating the hallowed kitchen. I had always been interested in 'things that go bump in the night' and one 'gift' a person could lay claim to without being branded too much of a crank was the reading of tea leaves. We decided to test our knowledge of human nature…

We collected about half the marrows, took them to the Stores and made our plans. At ten o'clock, at our request, Olly brought us tea from the Sergeants' Mess. The Airmen's Mess tea, ever mysterious, left a brown sludge in the bottom of one's cup. This was darkly referred to as Bromide but we didn't know if it was true! The Sergeants' Mess tea, we knew, would contain real tea leaves, whatever container Olly might bring it in.

We sat on a pile of sack close to the open door of the Officers' Mess kitchen, drinking our tea and Kath said in a loud voice,

"Will you tell our tea cups for us, June?"

"I'll try," I said, "I think I might have the 'fluence today."

Olly had gone and Muriel kept a weather eye on the growing crowd by the door as I made a great show of predicting the future for my colleagues. I didn't profess to being any good at it but had picked up a few pointers from Mom and various Aunts. No-one was more surprised than I was if any of my predictions came true!

I finished the performance, pretending not to notice the crowd by the door. We went back to work and Olly came later to take us to the geese enclosure.

That afternoon, whilst we collected the remaining marrows, we were cordially invited to go into the Officers' Mess kitchen and plied with tea, cakes and biscuits. After a decent interval the inevitable happened – I was asked to read the teacups of anyone who believed – and that meant everyone!

The twenty-four goslings duly arrived and we were thrilled with them. They were very handsome birds, with their snow white feathers and deep golden bills. They were put into the enclosure where there was a run and some cover and Sarge told us that we were to take turns of a week each to break up stale bread for them. This involved sitting in a large cubby-hole just off the Airmen's Mess kitchen, breaking up the bread, putting it into a large box and taking it to the enclosure each morning where Sarge was making a mash. The birds were quite cute to begin with but sadly, like humans, they lost their charm as they grew into adulthood. Individual characteristics began to show themselves. There were bullies and the bullied, leaders and followers, the lazy and the active Geese could, as Olly had warned us, be very vicious indeed. They were to cause us many headaches in the course of the next few months and we hadn't given a thought to what their ultimate fate might be. We regarded them as mischievous pets, a welcome diversion from the vegetables.

A field alongside the enclosure had been planted with cabbage and on one occasion when we were busy with hoeing, a charming man came to talk to us. He was the Church of England padre, a Mr Williams, who was billeted in the village with his family. He was most concerned with our welfare and said that if we needed advice of any sort we should go to him. We assured him politely that we had no complaints at all and had always been treated with respect. Our position was in fact quite unique. We were accepted as three responsible girls doing a useful job of work and we got on well with most people. There were three padres on camp – Mr Williams, Mr Swann the Canadian padre and Father Edwards, a Catholic Father. We had heard that Mr Swann's sermons were really good and that he would be preaching in the village church in the near future. We decided that all being well at home we would stay on camp that weekend to hear him. We hadn't yet seen the inside of the church, only the pub next to it!

It was inevitable that we should have our favourites, not only amongst the geese but the flyers too. It was at one of the village dances that we met a crew in training, with whom we would become great friends. There was Ken MacDonald, the pilot, a Canadian, dark-haired with a neat moustache, dependable and quietly spoken, father figure to the rest of the crew. There was Johnny, the observer, fair-haired and enigmatic, and Carl the grey-haired navigator who said he was ten years younger than he looked. There was craggy faced Jack, the bomb aimer, and lastly 'Irish', the only non-Canadian. He was the rear gunner and the youngest member of the crew. We spent many happy hours together dancing at the village hall or having a drink at the King's Head. After their course was completed they and their contemporaries would be going on operations and we tried not to think of that time. We tried to be cheerful company for the boys and it was a pleasure having them as friends.

On the Sunday before Bill Brock, our American friend was due to leave Honeybourne camp Kath said, as we travelled back to Stratford-upon-Avon, "Shall I make myself scarce, June, when we get to Stratford? You know Bill would like to be alone with you."

I looked at her with dismay, "Oh no! He's nice and he's generous but I don't care for him in that way, Kath. Don't you dare leave me!"

I had suspected that Bill had grown fond of me even though we had never been alone together. What applied on camp applied out of too – we three girls never made individual dates. Kath saw that I was adamant and agreed to stay. As the bus arrived at the car park of the pub, which served as a bus terminus, we could see Bill and I felt a little guilty.

"Good old Bill," Kath chuckled, "He's got his green bag with him."

We had been eternally grateful to Bill for many items which he'd bought for us at the PX, the American equivalent of the NAAFI. Soap, toothpaste, sweets, cigarettes and other things which would have cost us a large slice of our wages. It was Bill who introduced us to the sweet with the hole in the middle, then called Lifesavers. Over a last glass of ginger wine in the pub we said goodbye to Bill and one of his friends, Ben, who had joined us. We would miss Bill very much, for he had raised our perception of Americans way above gum chewing level. We both promised him we would write to him, or see him if he ever came to Birmingham although I didn't want to give him encouragement.

Most of our time at Wellesbourne camp had been happy but there were also sad times. One night as we walked up the lane we heard a plane circling, as was usual. Suddenly, we heard a tremendous crash. "Oh god!" Kath gasped, and we hung on to one another in fear. In the morning we found out that Ken and his crew were safe; another crew in training had died tragically. We had felt so helpless.

Muriel spent one night a week writing to her family and friends although she wrote to Ian every day. When Kath and I were invited to go to the Memorial Theatre we decided to break our rule, advising Muriel to lock her door. We cycled to the main gate where our escorts John and Alan, who were maintenance officers, were waiting. They had suggested that we cycle to Stratford-upon-Avon on a back road as there would be less traffic. I was still new to cycling and was quite relieved.

The evening was very enjoyable. The production was a farce called 'Sleeping Out' which we had never heard of but it was funny and made a change from the cinema. During this excursion both of my cycle tyres developed punctures but finances being what they were I knew I would have to ride round on the rims for a while, taking care not to let Sarge or the Squadron Leader see me!

Now that we had conned our way into the Officers' Mess kitchen we were never short of a drink or a snack wherever we happened to be working. We were quite well organised now – giant sausage rolls from the Sergeants' Mess, toast and butter from the Airmen's Mess and cheese sandwiches or cakes courtesy of exalted cooks of the Officers' Mess kitchen. Tea breaks were very pleasant indeed.

When Sarge was not on camp we made a beeline for the Officers' Mess kitchen, savouring the ever-present smell of kidneys, eggs and bacon. Of course the price of admission was the inevitable teacup reading and I was becoming quite adept at forecasting (or inventing) rosy futures for the ever-optimistic cooks!

The marrows had been weighed in at Stores and already consumed in the Sergeants' or Officers' Messes so we never had the chance of tasting one. Potato lifting was almost upon us and we were likely to become heartily sick of 'them spuds' as Sarge called them.

Although the Wellington bomber had become a familiar sight to us we had thought it unlikely that we would ever see the inside of one. However, one day, Ken said, "Would you like to see the inside of A for Apple?"

"Oh could we, Ken?" We were delighted but doubted if the powers that be would allow it. Somehow Ken arranged it for us.

I had always imagined that a bomber gave adequate protection to its crew but as we all climbed the ladder into the belly of A for Apple we were in for a shock. To our inexperienced eyes protection seemed very inadequate. The framework consisted of criss-cross pieces of metal backed by a fabric which looked no stronger than paper. My heart sank very low as Ken proudly showed us the instrument panel, the gun turret, the bomb aimer's, navigator's and observer's seats. He let us sit in each seat, no longer technical details to be read about, but places to be taken in an identical plane by dear friends over enemy territory. We showed as much enthusiasm as we could muster but deep down I felt great fear for Ken and his crew, and their brave contemporaries. I'm sure Kath and Muriel did too at that moment.

One day we were working in the cabbage field near the enclosure. Fog was lying low on the ground and Sarge was driving the tractor with a barrow attached, across the adjoining field. He told us to follow with buckets, pick up stones and dump them at the side of the field. Not only was it difficult to see a hand in front of us but also ran the risk of being run down by Sarge's erratic tractoring. However, after he'd taken the tractor away and the fog had lifted we became aware of a tall dark young man in officer's uniform leaning on a gate, watching us. We viewed him discreetly from behind a pile of stones.

"Admin type," I said knowingly.

"Some big-wig's nephew come to sit out the war here," was Kath's opinion. But we were both wrong. The young officer was Wing Commander John B. Tait, already much decorated and later to be awarded the VC for leading the attack on the German battleship 'Tirpitz.' His spell as Commanding Officer of Wellesbourne Mountford camp was to be his rest period, as he had completed 87 operations to date. Later he married the WAAF CO, both in full uniform and their photograph was in the Birmingham Post.

We greatly admired the flyers and our admiration increased tenfold after seeing the inside of A for Apple. One night, after a raid on Germany, a Lancaster bomber landed on one of the runways, having run out of fuel. We cycled over to see it and felt very insignificant indeed as we looked up into the bomb bay which was open, two bombs still in place. Having four engines the plane looked a lot more substantial than the Wellington which had only two. Nevertheless it still gave me the shivers…

One night Ken said, "Is it this weekend you're staying?" We told him it was as we wanted to hear Mr Swann's sermon at the village church on the Sunday. He said, "Have you got time to come and help me choose a birthday present for my mother? I would be grateful."

"We'd love to," I said. Muriel was going to a family wedding in Coventry on the Saturday so Kath and I arranged to go with Ken and the crew to Stratford-upon-Avon by bus. Muriel said she would be back in time for the service. The crew had never been to Stratford-upon-Avon and were anxious to see Shakespeare's birth place before they left the camp. We found Henley Street, following a crowd of American soldiers who were being shown round by a very knowledgeable, very proud grey-haired lady. We learned that this had once been two houses. In one William had been born and in the other his father conducted his business.

None of us could imagine what the Bard would have thought of all these American accents and flashing light bulbs.

There was a lovely English garden at the back of the house and we spent a very pleasant afternoon. Kath and I helped Ken choose a scarf for his mother and we all had tea at the Judith Shakespeare Restaurant in the town. We returned to camp tired but happy and later made our way to the village hall dance. Mrs Vale, one of the ladies who served refreshments had already offered Muriel the chance of a room if we decided to leave the hut. It would only remain for Kath and myself to find somewhere and Mrs Vale gave us names and addresses of people who would be willing to take us in.

Ken and the boys arrived later and over tea and sandwiches they told us more about the Canadians and their daily lives. They were so keen, so anxious to give their best.

The following morning, Sunday, Kath and I went down to the Waafery for breakfast. It was true! There was bacon and a real shell egg for breakfast! How we enjoyed it!

We stayed in the hut for the rest of the morning doing some repairs and I prepared my blue C & A dress for the next social occasion which would be the Corporals' dance at the NAAFI. A new NAAFI was being built on the camp and was almost finished.

My wardrobe was still not extensive. I had a black crepe dress the same style as the blue, from C & A Modes in Corporation Street. On both I rang the changes with half a yard of frilling bought from Woolworth's, or sometimes wore an artificial rose at the neck. I also had my 'best' black and white dress given to me by my glamourous Aunt Doll.

Later Muriel arrived and we sat talking and eating peanuts which Bill Brock had brought us from the PX. In the early evening we put on our best walking out uniforms and set off to meet Ken and the crew outside the church. There was almost a full congregation already but we managed to get seats. Some people had to stand outside the open door to hear Mr Swann's sermon. As he delivered his sermon we understood why he was so popular with the Canadians and with the villagers too. After the service we all went to the church canteen and had tea, cheese sandwiches and lardy cakes.

The following day we saw the Squadron Leader and told him that we had all found digs, and how much we would be paying.

"Very good," he said. "I will increase your salaries by ten shillings a week each."

We couldn't believe our good luck – we would be better of by four shillings a week! Muriel had also had trouble persuading Mrs Vale to charge but in the end she too had suggested a shilling a night.

On the strength of my newfound wealth I ordered two new cycle tyres for the WAAF issue bike from the local garage at four shillings each! I would be able to ride round camp with a clear conscience again!

A few days later Sarge said, "Go down to the Sergeants' Mess. There's a carrier bike you can borer for yer move."

"Oh thanks Sarge, that will be useful!" We were delighted and not a little surprised at his co-operation!

At the next Sergeants' dance Don Harrison came over to give us a firm date for our photo session.

"Will it be all right with the officer in charge?" I asked. He grinned, "Of course! He's longing to meet you all. Seven o'clock then, next Wednesday night." He gave us instructions how to get to the Photographic Department and the next day as we cut cabbages we discussed what we would wear. I decided on the black and white dress given to me by my Aunt Doll, and Kath and Muriel decided on dark dresses too.

The following Wednesday we had our evening meal, bathed and changed into our dresses, putting on a little more make-up than usual. In a state of excitement we dressed each other's hair and set out on our bikes for the Photographic Department. It was a hive of activity. There were flyers coming in and out carrying papers, WAAFS hanging washing on a line, others carrying mugs of coffee and tea. A radio was playing 'Silver Wings in the Moonlight' as Don came from a back room. He introduced us to his officer, Flying Officer Aylward, who sat at his desk reading a book, oblivious to the noise. He didn't seem to mind us at all!

Don took us into the studio, the spotlights already set up. Although we had all had Polyfotos done at a city store at one time or another none of us had been in a proper studio since childhood. Don photographed Muriel first then Kath, taking them out for coffee whilst he took half a dozen poses of me, much to my embarrassment. He said it was good practice for him for after the war.

We nicknamed our digs 'The Swinging Hovis' after hearing a mysterious creaking noise under our window the first night. It turned out to be a 'Teas-Hovis' sign, a relic of the house's role as a pre-war café for cyclists. I was able to enjoy three more nights of newfound comfort before finding myself in Sick Bay. I'd been helping lift sacks of potatoes onto the truck and suddenly fell down in pain, unable to move. Luckily I was already on the truck so Sarge drove me to Sick Quarters where a female doctor diagnosed a straining abdomen! The charming MO happened to be on leave so I was spared more embarrassment!

I spent ten days flat on my back in a ward along with a dozen WAAFS whose complaints ranged from 'flu to sprained ankles. By the time I was well enough to leave they were at least saying 'good morning'!

What made my stay really memorable was when Sarge sent me, with the girls, one of the last bunches of black grapes, cut by his own fair hand! I was more than a little surprised.

We were very happy in our new digs. It made the world of difference being able to sleep at night without being muffled up in extra clothes or having a light flashed into our eyes at three in the morning.

The routine worked well. Mr Ireland, who had a little job at Charlecote Hall, knocked on our door as he went out in the morning. We then had a quick cold wash in the water brought up by Mrs Ireland the previous night, in a flowered bowl with a matching jug. We cycled to the corner of Kineton Road to meet Muriel, thence to camp or to the Waafery for breakfast. We had our own front door key but were usually in by eleven.

I hadn't seen a great deal of Mom since joining the Land Army because of her shift work at Hollymoor, and we had to snatch available moments when we could. The following Saturday I went straight from the city centre to the hospital hoping I would see her for a few minutes before she went on duty otherwise we wouldn't see one another at all that weekend. It was lovely to have up-to-date news of the family; two of my aunts and uncles now had telephones and Mom was able to ring them from home occasionally.

After saying goodbye to Mom I went up to Sister Jones' ward on the first floor where I spent the afternoon talking as usual to lonely patients. There seemed to be an air of optimism amongst the men and I was pleased. The Second Front was being talked about more and more so perhaps the end of the war was in sight, in Europe anyway. The Far East was a separate and on-going war, a dreadful ordeal for our brave men and women.

As Sister Jones gave me tea and cake she said, "I don't know what I would have done without your help, June, especially with the French."

There had been no more accidents but there was always evidence of poor landings, skid marks on runways and hedges flattened or broken. If a pilot made a bad landing he was sent up again without delay.

Then something terrible happened… A good friend of Ken's, another Canadian named Gerry was an instructor at the station, having completed many operations in his time. Round his twinkling blue eyes he wore the scars of the time he tried to land a plane in the Mediterranean Sea after he'd told his crew to bale out! Whenever anyone asked him to relate the story he would say, "I couldn't leave my Kitty, could I?"

One night in the King's Head in Wellesbourne, he remarked casually, "There's a Wellington US down at Bristol. I've got to fly a maintenance crew down. I'll be back in a few days. See you then, ladies!"

A week passed and we hadn't seen Gerry or Ken and the crew. We began to wonder what had happened, and then one evening, as we went again to the King's Head we saw Ken sitting alone at a table. He was as white as a sheet and we just knew something terrible must have happened. But how could we ask him? And then he saw us and said bleakly, "It's Gerry… I hate to tell you but… he's dead." My heart turned over and Kath and Muriel must have felt the same.

"Oh, Ken!" We were close to tears, all of us.

Kath whispered, "What happened to Ken?"

He swallowed trying to keep his voice steady. It was awful to see him suffering.

"They had reached Bristol safely. The maintenance crew did the repairs on the other Wellington… They took two more days then Gerry… took off… they crashed in the sea. No-one survived…" Impulsively I put a hand on his. He was trembling… Just then the rest of the crew came in with a navigator who the girls knew as Tommy. His right hand was heavily bandaged and his face was fraught with emotion.

"God, Ken… I should have been Gerry's navigator! And… what did I do, for God's sake?" He held up his bandaged hand…

"I shut this in the bloody safe door, didn't I?"

Johnny, Ken's navigator said quietly, "Tom, your number hadn't come up!"

He made it sound so simple… Life and death had to be translated into simple terms if these men were to survive without losing their minds…

I looked at them now, hating war and everything about it.

Ken shook his head.

"June, we haven't got time to grieve."

Johnny wanted to buy us all a drink but we got up to go. The men needed to be on their own…

Kath and I took Muriel to Mrs Vale's house, where she was now lodging. She hadn't spoken at all and we guessed that she was thinking about her fiancé, Ian who was in Italy.

Arriving at our digs we just said goodnight to Mr and Mrs Ireland gently refusing a cup of cocoa which we usually had. The old couple were so kind and we still couldn't get over the charge she was making – one shilling a night which included the cocoa, a hot water bottle and a jug and bowl in the early morning. We took breakfast on camp, in the Airmen's Mess.

There were only two weeks left before Ken, Johnny, Carl and Jack, with a new observer would be leaving. Poor 'Irish' became air sick and was broken-hearted, convinced he had brought bad luck to the crew. Ken had put in a successful request that 'Irish' should be allowed to stay with the crew wherever they might find themselves. It would be an operational station. We had long since realised that Ken (MacDonald, Canadian of a Scottish ancestry) was highly respected throughout the camp and by the powers that be.

On their final Saturday night a dance was organised by the local Council to be held at the Corn Exchange in Leamington Spa. Personnel and their guests were being transported in flight buses so in a fever of excitement we put on dresses (we each only had one with us!) and made up our faces with our limited stock of make-up kindly given to us by the girls of the NAAFI!

We had discovered in a little shop in our hometown, Birmingham, a little jointed man in wood, painted in bright colours and decided to give it to Ken as their mascot, if they hadn't got one already. It was with sadness mixed with excitement that we travelled with Ken and the crew to Leamington. Kath and Muriel had already given me the task of making a little speech as we presented the little man to Ken.

The first half of the evening went with a swing, with us doing the Palais Glide and 'Underneath the Spreading Chestnut Tree' much to the amusement of the Canadian boys. Then in the interval, when we could have a hot drink or alcohol I opened my hand bag and took out the little pink oblong box which had contained some Coty make-up.

Johnny laughed, "What's this then?"

Shyly I opened the box and handed the lower part to Ken. He stared at the object for a moment then slowly picked it up from its bed of cotton wool.

"Ken," I began, "we saw him in a little shop in Birmingham one Friday night when we arrived back for the weekend. We thought... we thought..." I stopped, swallowing hard. I didn't want to cry at this point in time!

Muriel piped up, "It's a mascot, Ken, for your next plane!"

"Thank-you, my dear girls! You don't know what this means to me! June..." He turned and looked at me and I thought, 'Oh please God, keep them all safe!"

Kath said, "It would be great if you could let us know how you all are from time to time Ken."

"We'll try," he said. He looked at the little figure again. "I think we'll christen him Joe, if the rest of these guys agree."

"Yes! Yes!" was the general reply.

Ken said, "I shall hang him on my instrument panel. June... bless you all, my dear ladies of the soil!"

The last part of the evening was more subdued but it suited all of us.

We met the boys for the last time and had a drink in the King's Head. I'd got Mom's Brownie camera so was able to take a photograph of the crew all together including 'Irish.'

We would miss them very much and we worked with a deep sense of loss, and were apprehensive about their futures; but were unable to put it into words to one another.

About twelve months after the end of the war I was ill in bed with 'flu. I heard the post come and then Mom opened the door to someone. I couldn't hear what was said but after she closed the door Mom called up, "June! You've got a parcel... from Canada!"

"I'm coming down!"

I heard her footsteps on the stairs and she came in carrying the parcel. My heart thumped when I saw the stamp. It was from Canada! Mom handed it to me and watched my face as I wrestled with the wrapping.

It was a gift of chocolates. Before I opened the letter I knew it must be from Ken or one of his crew.

I read Ken's letter, 'Joe' had taken them safely there and back on two tours of ops he'd written and he'd met up with Johnny back in Canada.

Mom said, "Flyers are very superstitious. Soldiers had lucky mascots in World War I."

"Did Dad have anything to bring him luck?" I asked.

She kissed my cheek. "Just our prayers… I like to think they helped."

"I'm sure they did! Bless you Mom." I said.

I looked at her serene face and knew that I was extremely privileged having such a wonderful mother.

⸙ Poems ⸙

I STILL HAVE A DREAM

Although in my eighties I still have a dream
that war is no more and peace reigns supreme,
that men with their power will see common sense,
use passion, compassion, not sit on their fence.
That cruelty and envy will no longer bring tears
and the sound of men marching will no longer cause fears.

But we ordinary people have more than one dream,
Forever embracing our families so dear.
Could not the world's rulers have respect for life's scheme
and banish their pride, bring pity to bear?

MEMORIES

All those old memories – still they return,
Bread from a basket, milk from a churn.
Blue bags of sugar, butter in slabs,
Sherbet and licorice and caramel dabs.
Love hearts with messages, colours so bright.
Excitement in making and flying a kite.
Hopscotch and yo-yo, a whip and a top,
A ha'penny to spend in Cameron's shop.
Swings and a maypole, sheds in the park,
Nightlights at bedtime, fear of the dark.

Pictures on tins of the Queen and the King,
Gas mantles fragile as butterfly wing.
Cod liver oil and malt in a jar,
Making a wish on a bright falling star.
Syrup of figs, toothpaste in tins,
Knitting a dishcloth on big wooden pins.
Catswhisker radio, music and news,
Other girls' shiny black ankle strap shoes...

Dandelion clocks, bluebells in woods,
School friends in colourful mac capes with hoods.
Cinema crush on Saturday morn,
New pennies in socks at Christmas Day dawn.
We watched from a bridge as a horse pulled a barge,
Not knowing just then that the world was so large...

What is this mystery – what does it mean?
Memories so vivid – memories so green?